Ramón A. Sierra

A HANDBOOK FOR DISCIPLESHIP TRAINING

Copyright © 2013 Ramòn A. Sierra

Published by
Global Nazarene Publications
17001 Praire Star Parkway
Lenexa, KS 66220 E.U.A.

All rights reserved

ISBN 978-1-56344-768-6

Page concept and design: Jerson Chupina

You have permission to copy and adapt the "Focusing" sections of each less as well as the appendixes
for non-commercial puposes in the local church.

Table of Contents

Dedication 5

Forward 7

Presentation 9

Introduction to Discipleship Training 11

Lesson 1: What is a disciple of Jesus? 15

Lesson 2: Biblical foundations for discipleship 21

Lesson 3: Discipleship as Christian spiritual formation 29

Lesson 4: Discipleship as a means of multiplication and small groups 35

Lesson 5: Discipleship for pastors 41

Lesson 6: Discipleship for everybody 47

Lesson 7: Discipleship in the family 52

Lesson 8: Discipleship strategy for the local church 58

Lesson 9: Using discipleship materials 65

Lesson 10: How to develop a discipleship ministry 73

End Notes 79

Appendices 83

Dedication

I dedicate this work with great affection and a profound sense of debt to three faithful women disciples of Jesus that have impacted my life in an indelible way. They are:

Angelita Montoyo Santiago, my grandmother
Miriam Mastache de Sierra, my mother
Blanca D. Campos Ríos, my wife

I owe them much of what I am and the way I have developed various ministries that have been under my responsibility throughout these 33 years. Each one of them showed me different aspects of what it means to follow Christ.

From my beloved grandma, Angelita, I received my inspiration and human model of total surrender and self-giving service to people. In January 1994 she went on to enjoy the heavenly mansions. Miriam, my mom, who went to be with the Lord in July 2010, guided my tender steps as a child towards Jesus from our home to church, impressing upon me a special love for the church. Together with Blanquita, my fellow companion of the Way, we have ministered throughout the years and she has helped me in the process, contributing in different ways from the intimacy of our marriage to my growth as an authentic disciple of Jesus. I love all three of them with all my heart.

Thanks, sisters, disciples of the Master, you have discipled me through your lives and wise counsel! What a blessing to have you in the path of the Kingdom! Only God will be able to reward you as you deserve.

Forward

Obedience to Jesus' commandment to make disciples does not happen automatically. Effective discipleship requires intentionality and determined focused efforts. Understanding the basic and fundamental principles of disciple-making is best achieved if someone teaches and models the foundational concepts.

People often ask, "What can I use to train others for productive disciple-making? Ramón Sierra has produced a valuable resource that precisely answers that question. *A Handbook for Discipleship Training* provides ten essential lessons that are invaluable for training others in the great challenge of how to make disciples. It addresses the broad spectrum of needs and issues faced by local churches, pastors and small group leaders.

This training handbook provides useful tools and materials, strategies and practices that can be implemented in the local church. This well researched guidebook equips church and family leaders to not only live in obedience to the Great Commission, but to also reproduce that obedience in the lives of those they serve.

Ramón Sierra's life and work are well reflected in these instructions for being a disciple of Jesus, learning from Him and obeying Him, then intentionally modeling how to teach others to know and follow Jesus in the same way.

I pray that your ministry will be enriched and will result in much fruit to the glory of God as you utilize this significant discipleship training resource.

Dr. Woodie Steven
Church of the Nazarene
Global Director Sunday School and Discipleship Ministries International

We thank God for the opportunity of witnessing of the great blessing we received through this discipleship training material. We never imagined that through this material the life of our church would be motivated, but above all, we were confronted with the need of making disciples.

We are aware that our mission is "to make Christlike disciples in the nations", but I believe that many times those are pretty words that do not transcend. Through this course, we were challenged to fulfill this great commission. This task is not easy because it requires that we invest time, money and effort. But I believe this is what it really means to be disciples: deny ourselves, take up his cross every day and follow him; dying to our bad habits, to our "ego" and dedicating our lives to the Lord in worship and service.

In our local church, with God's help and through Sunday School, we have designed a discipleship system for children, young people and adults. We are expanding this system one step at a time, but God is blessing this precious initiative in many ways.

Thank you brother Ramón, you have put in our hands more than a course, a vision, that I believe comes from heaven, as the desire of God´s heart.

> Rev. Marcos Galicia Rodríguez
> Pastor Church of the Nazarene
> Toluca, State of Mexico

In 2007 a group of leaders from our churches attended a discipleship training time in Villaflores, Chiapas, Mexico guided by our missionary Ramón Sierra. After two days of training and motivation we returned to our area of work with the enthusiasm of sharing what we had received with other brothers and sisters from our local churches.

Little by little we began to form discipleship groups in various churches of our zone. Fifty two leaders signed up and participated in prayer, fellowship and studying some themes related to discipleship. In 2008, with the greater part of these persons we started the School of Timothies, where we continued studying monthly directed by selected teachers. In January 2009 we graduated 25 students from this project.

At the present, we continue working with discipleship in this manner. We are preparing so that leadership classes may begin in each one of our churches. Already in one congregation we have 22 persons that meet for weekly classes. But besides this, discipleship in the churches and the School of Timothies have provided the foundations to open two new theological by extension centers with 16 students in the basic level and 16 more students at the degree level (post-graduate studies before the masters level).

An important part of the impulse for this whole process was our experience of the discipleship training, the material you now have in your hands. It is our desire that through this discipleship training God may initiate in your church or churches a process similar to the one he has work with us!

> Rev. Manuel Molina
> Superintendent Sierra District
> Chiapas, Mexico

Presentation

Welcome to this time together around the theme of discipleship that could revolutionize your walk with Christ and change the direction of the church. This is our hope and prayer.

This basic discipleship training is initially oriented to trainers, men and women, young and old, followers of Jesus in the Church, committed and with the necessary gifts to disciple others. All of this with the local church as the central objective for Christian discipleship, since it is the local church where we will focus everything we do in this time of learning.

The training you will receive in these days is comprehensive and intense. In this discipleship experience, although there will be lectures, we will utilize the small group process. In the small groups you will share devotional times, exercises in each lesson, so you will have the opportunity to establish close friendships and spiritual support beyond the training time.

The lessons aim to provide basic tools for carrying out the realization of an intentional, dynamic and life-long discipleship ministry.

Each lesson contains:

- A lesson summary at the beginning with the general objective and the key Bible verses to memorize.

- Group exercises scattered throughout the lesson and at the end an integration exercise.

- After each lesson you will find a sheet titled *Focusing* to go deeper in one aspect of the lesson.

With the necessary adjustments, this material can also be used for training local discipleship leaders, and thus provide solid foundations for this ministry. Also, this same material can be used as lessons to teach the local congregation, whether it be as Bible studies, Sunday School classes or in small groups for adults or young people during various months. Each lesson can be divided into more lessons depending on the time available.

At the end of this material in the appendix is included an evaluation sheet to be used at the end of each lesson or at the end of the training time.

This material can also be shared with a group of pastors and leaders of various churches, zones or districts. They in turn would train leaders in the local churches. The schedule is flexible, depending on your needs. It can be taught over an intense weekend, at least three days, weekly, monthly, or spread out over a semester.

Apart from all that the student will learn, the most significant thing about this training is what happens after the class is over. To build the bridge between this training and the local church we will conclude with a conversation among the participants of each district to initiate a strategy that will help churches in their discipleship ministry.

As part of this strategy—that later on should be developed with greater detail—a discipleship coordinator (either by district, zones, or a group of churches) can be appointed. This coordinator should facilitate the reproduction of this training and based on what has been a learned, put in place mechanisms to evaluate and accompany each local church in the process of effectively developing their discipleship ministry.

This training could be the "mustard seed" that God can use so that our existing churches and the new ones to be planted can become communities of disciples that carry out the mission of the Master: make disciples in all the nations. This requires that we begin the process, knowing that it will not be easy. We must be persistent in the task and sensitive to the voice of the Spirit. We will not see instantaneous fruits, "for at the proper time we will reap (a great harvest) if we do not give up" (Galatians 6:9, NIV).

Let us begin together this training time with joy, great expectations and our willingness to let Jesus continue to shape us as His authentic disciples so we can then touch the lives of others!

Introduction to Discipleship Training

General Objective

Share with the trainers a general orientation and launch the challenge of the urgent need of a discipleship ministry in each local church.

Lesson Summary

- Worship time together.
- Welcome and organize participants into small groups.
- Mission and vision of the discipleship ministry of the Church of the Nazarene in the Mesoamerica Region: Mexico, the Caribbean, Central America.
- Focus and seven objectives of this Discipleship Training.
- Format of the training sessions
- Discipleship Challenge: exerpt of the report of the Board of General Superintendents to the General Board of the International Church of the Nazarene in February 2006.

Key verse to memorize

"They devoted themselves to the apostles' teaching and to the fellowship, to the breaking of bread and to prayer. Every day they continued to meet together in the temple courts. They broke bread in their homes and ate together with glad and sincere hearts, praising God and enjoying the favor of all the people. And the Lord added to their number daily those who were being saved." (Acts 2:42, 46-47, NIV).

Opening: Prayer and Worship Time.

I. Welcome to this training: a discipleship experience

This is training for trainers, for leaders committed to the mission of the church.

II. Organization of small groups

Group exercise

So that the participants may get to know each other by doing the exercise on the *Focusing* sheet at the end of the lesson.

III. Mission and vision of the Discipleship Ministry of the Church is to create a system to help each local church in its discipleship ministry as it...

- studies its biblical bases.
- presents a basic strategy that motivates a local discipleship strategy.
- offers personal support, counsel and training (team of leaders).
- develops materials and tools together.
- provides a space to share and improve.
- establishes a solid foundation for leadership development.

IV. Focus of this discipleship training

This training should be by invitation only. Participants become part of a small, mixed group of leaders of each district, zone or community to form a team of trainers in discipleship ministry for the local churches.

Seven objectives for this training

1. Have a discipleship experience—grow in a disciple-making way of life.
2. Rediscover the biblical and practical foundations of discipleship that should be reflected in the type of church, pastor and ministry we need today.
3. Share knowledge, tools and experiences.
4. Create awareness of the urgent need of a dynamic discipleship ministry in each local church.
5. Form a team of trainers that can develop an effective discipleship ministry in each local church.
6. Be acquainted with and know how to use materials, strategy and available resources for the local discipleship ministry.
7. Elaborate an implementation strategy for this training, taking into consideration the foundations we have studied and the needs in the discipleship ministry in the churches.

V. Format to follow

- This handbook provides all the material in writing.
- The teacher will share the lessons and carry out the learning activities.
- Small groups will be used at all times.
- Sharing questions and experiences around discipleship will be welcomed.
- Go over the program and time allotments.

VI. An excerpt from the report of the Board of General Superintendents to the General Board of the International Church of the Nazarene in February 2006 prepared by Dr. Jerry Porter

We celebrate the nearly 700,000 new Nazarenes who have joined our church since 1999. Unfortunately, due to death

"We must give more attention to discipleship... the time has come to move beyond membership to discipleship."

JERRY PORTER

Group Exercise

Trust Walk: Pair up in twos, preferably men with men and women with women. One of the persons should close their eyes or cover their eyes with a handkerchief. He/She will be guided by other person that can see around the room and surrounding areas. You can give verbal instructions and hold on to the person, if you would like. After a few minutes you will trade places.

Reflection after the experience: What did you feel when you were being guided? What did you feel when you were guiding your partner? What does this exercise teach us about discipleship?

or removal, during these six years we lost two of every three who joined our denominational family.

We must give more attention to discipleship. What does it mean to be a disciple of Jesus Christ? It is to be a continual student of Jesus—guided, instructed, and helped by the Lord through fellow believers in every aspect of our life; reproducing other disciples as a natural part of our total devotion to Christ.

... the time has come to move beyond membership to discipleship. The goal is not to make believers, or even members, but to make disciples. That was the mission of Jesus, and it is our declared mission as well.

Author and Wesley scholar Mike Henderson insists that we have things turned around. "Jesus said, 'I will build my church. You make disciples.' Instead, we try to build the church; and who is making disciples?"

The real cost of discipling is investing time in someone's life—giving ourselves away. It means spending more time with fewer people, the basic principle taught by Christ.

These new disciples are nurtured into mentoring relationships that lead to spiritually disciplined lives. If these new disciples do not become strong disciples, much of the increase will dissipate.

We can no longer justify carelessness in assimilating new believers. New Methodist converts were immediately assimilated into small groups where they were discipled and taught the way of Christian perfection. This is our Wesleyan heritage.

Those needed for mission and ministry are within the sound of our voices. It is our joy and responsibility to disciple, equip, and empower them to be the new generation of spiritual and servant leaders.

In his book, The Cost of Discipleship, Dietrich Bonhoeffer writes: "Christianity without discipleship is Christianity without Christ." Evangelism and making disciples go together. Our future is bright as we develop spiritual leaders who will reproduce themselves and multiply their effectiveness. Whether it's one-on-one or groups of 3, 7, or 12, John Wesley's call for spiritual accountability among believers is relevant and urgently needed for our day!

We can and we must close the back door of the Church of the Nazarene. We dare not be careless with the precious new believers. By God's grace we will become churches that learn to multiply disciples through intentional relationships, accountability, and participation in ministry. We will multiply disciples by multiplying leaders, small groups, and new congregations. With the Lord's help we will judge our personal and collective fruitfulness by how effectively we make disciples.

Note: In 2007, the international leaders of the Church of the Nazarene summarized their mission statement with the following phrase: "To Make Christlike Disciples in the Nations."

"Christianity without discipleship is Christianity without Christ."

DIETRICH BONHOEFFER

Integration Activity

What do you think about this report that speaks to the Church of the Nazarene around the world? What feelings, concerns and reactions does this report provoke in you?

The International Church of the Nazarene is a denomination from the Wesleyan tradition and part of the Holiness Movement. It was founded in 1908 by Dr. Phineas Bresee, Methodist pastor, when various holiness groups merged in the USA. Their headquarters are in Lenexa, Kansas and the ministry extends to over 159 world areas. Dr. Jerry Porter is one of the six General Superintendents of the Church of the Nazarene.

Focusing...

Group dynamic: Getting to know each other

Give each participant a card of a different color and have them form a big circle. A signal will be made and everyone with the same color will form into a group and carry out the following activity:

- Each person will introduce him/herself, giving their name and sharing some interesting personal fact.

- They will choose a leader and a spokesperson, which will introduce all the members of the group and will share what the group has worked on.

- They will agree on a name for the group.

- The Epitaph: We have all visited a cemetery in some moment of our lives and without a doubt some epitaphs have caught our attention. They try to summarize the life of those persons. Let us imagine ourselves before our own tomb, how would you like your epitaph to read?

- Each person will write out their own epitaph following the model that is provided below. Share this in your group and choose one so you can share with everyone together.

- All the small groups will come together and the leader or the spokesperson will share what they have done in their small group:

    - Name of the group
    - Introduce the members
    - Epitaph chosen by the group

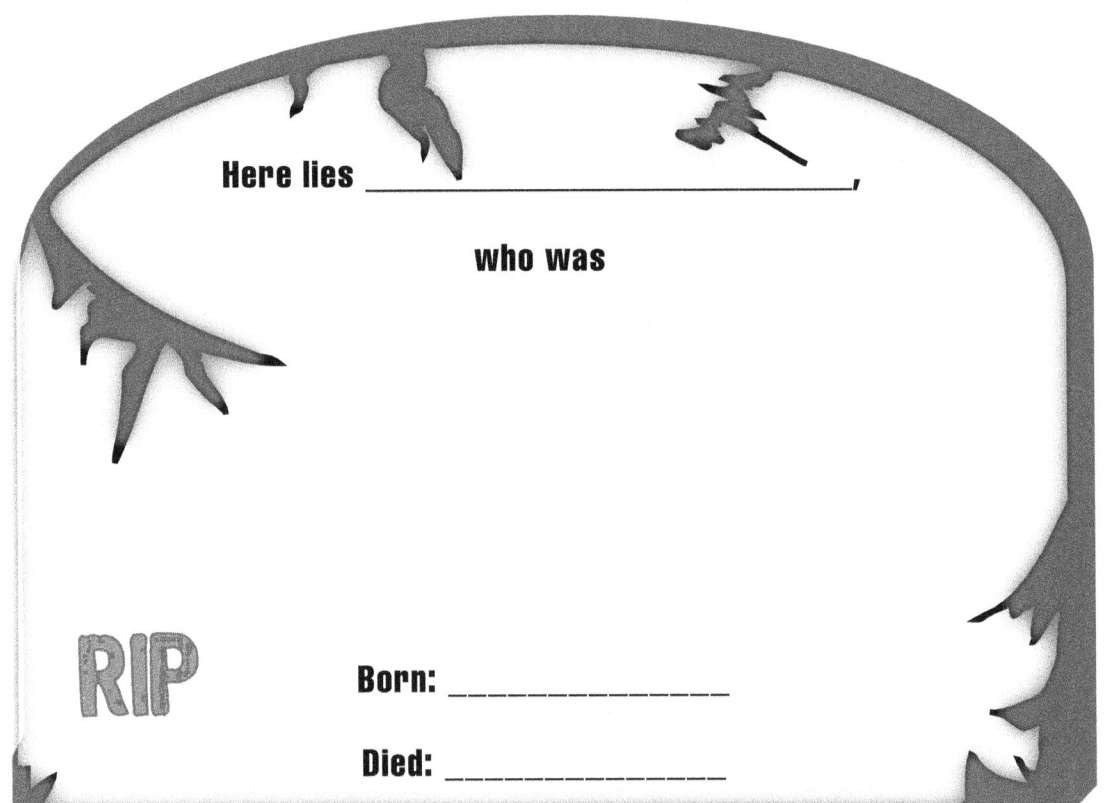

Lesson 1
What does it mean to be a disciple of Jesus?

General Objective

Provide criteria so that the trainers can define biblically and with precision what a disciple of Jesus is as a foundation for the discipleship ministry.

Lesson Summary

- Five perspectives of a disciple of Jesus.
- Reconciling various aspects of discipleship in the New Testament.
- Some key definitions.
- Indispensable and biblical elements for the local discipleship ministry.

Key verse to memorize

"The disciple is not above his master: but every one that is perfect shall be as his master." (Luke 6:40, KJV).

Introduction

Group Exercise

Each person writes down and shares his/her personal definition of a disciple of Jesus, and then create a group definition that will be shared with everyone together.

What does it mean to be a disciple of Jesus? The answer to this question is fundamental for in the church various perceptions co-exist. Our understanding of what a disciple of Jesus is will be reflected in the discipleship ministry carried out in the church, or in the lack of an intentional and organized discipleship ministry.

Bill Hull affirms that: "Understanding what a disciple is and what a disciple does are top priority for the church. The irony of the church is that we throw the word disciple around freely, but too often with no definition"[1] or with various definitions that can be confusing and even contradicting.

"Understanding what a disciple is and what a disciple does are top priority for the church".

BILL HULL

Many times, churches do not have a discipleship ministry, not because they ignore the topic, but because they have mistakenly...

- equated making disciples with evangelizing,
- have assumed that discipleship is simply the automatic result of people participating in the programs and activities of the church: having services, teaching, working with children and young people, evangelizing, etc.

I. Five perspectives of what a disciple of Jesus is [2]

1. Disciples as Learners

The term "disciple" refers to one who puts him/herself under the teaching authority of a great teacher, but it has no reference to whether or not the person is a Christian. Charles Ryrie describes a "disciple" as "a follower

Group Exercise

Five groups will be formed and each group will discuss the model of discipleship that is assigned to them. They will summarize the characteristics and possible limitations or difficulties of the focus of their model. Then they will share this with everyone.

of a teacher and his teachings, involving, in Bible times, traveling with that teacher wherever he went." [3]

This view is instructive because it emphasizes the early linguistic relationship between the noun "disciple" and the verb "learn." It underscores the relationship of teacher-disciple, the verbal instruction of the teacher regarding doctrine or principles, which should be learned, accepted and shared with others. We also find in the New Testament disciples of other teachers apart from Jesus: disciples of John the Baptist (John 1:35), of the Pharisees (Matthew 22:15-16) and of Moses (John 9:28).

This model has two basic difficulties. In the first place, the Greek term for "disciple" (*mathetes*) is used in Scripture in a manner different than simply to designate a "learner." A disciple of Jesus was much more than someone who learned concepts.

The second difficulty appears when we note the normal use of the term disciple in the book of Acts. In Acts the term is normally used without any qualifiers simply to designate "Christians" (Acts 11:26). To be a Christian and a disciple of Jesus in the New Testament was the same thing.

2. Disciples as Committed Believers

Juan Carlos Ortiz in his book *Disciple* answers the question "What is a disciple?" A disciple is one who follows Jesus Christ. But being Christians does not necessarily mean we are his disciples, even though we are members of his kingdom. Following Christ means acknowledging Him as Lord; it means serving Him as a slave." [4]

Another author similarly asserts that "there is a vast difference between being saved and being a disciple. Not all men who are saved are disciples although all who are disciples are saved. In discussing the question of discipleship, we are not dealing with a man's salvation. We are dealing with a man's relationship to Jesus Christ as his teacher, his Master, and his Lord." [5]

This discipleship model emphasizes Jesus' radical challenge to count the cost of discipleship. It points to the small group of disciples who followed Jesus and emphasizes that when they left all to follow Jesus, they became models of a higher spiritual calling. It compares Jesus' disciples with the crowds around Him, and concludes that the difference lies in responding to Jesus' call to commitment. The beginning point of discipleship, therefore, was commitment.

This model suggests that there are two levels within the church today: disciples and ordinary believers. A disciple is a more committed Christian than the average Christian. This model of discipleship is quite widespread, being found in several different forms. But we must ask, Is this what the New Testament teaches a disciple is?

This model also encounters difficulties. For example, when Jesus gives a message directed to the "crowds" which calls them to count the cost before they become His "disciples" (Lk. 14:25-33), or when He tells the rich young ruler to go give all his riches to the poor before he can enter into eternal life (Mt. 19:16-22), what is the spiritual nature of the crowds? of the rich young ruler? Are they already believers or not? Is it a call to deeper commitment, or a call to salvation? These texts seem to indicate that this is a call to salvation, since these persons were not yet disciples of Jesus. We should also remember that to be a believer and a disciple of Jesus are synonyms in the New Testament. To be a disciple of the Master was not a higher or optional level of following Jesus but the required norm for all his followers, which includes commitment from the beginning of their relationship with Christ.

3. Disciples as Ministers

A disciple is the believer who has been called out from among lay believers in order to enter into ministry. Discipleship means to be with Jesus in order to learn from Him how to serve the crowd, the church. They are those chosen and trained as successors to Jesus in His role as exorcist, healer, prophet, and teacher. [6]

This model results from observing the close relationship of the twelve disciples with Jesus in His ministry, and their later ministry to the early church. It concludes that the radical call to discipleship was intended to be a model of how a believer today is called into ministry.

This model, as the prior model, makes the same mistake of limiting the disciples to a selected group of the church, in this case, to pastors. A problem arises when a clear distinction is not made between the Twelve as *disciples* and the Twelve as *apostles*. The Twelve were always disciples, but in Acts they continue their discipleship process but as apostles, leaders in the newly born church.

4. Disciples as Converts and Discipleship comes later

Disciples are converts to Jesus, and then discipleship comes after that. A disciple is one who has been evangelized, and the later process of growth is called "perfecting" or "discipleship". [7] Once disciples are made, they then begin the lifetime road of discipleship.

This discipleship model emphasizes that the meaning of the Great Commission's imperative, "make disciples" of all the nations, is to make converts out of non-Christians. It stresses conversion as the beginning point of the Christian life, which means that conversion is the beginning point of becoming a disciple.

The difficulty with this model is that it seems to separate the imperative of the Great Commission, "make disciples," from the following participles, "baptizing" and "teaching." The discrepancy may lie in the use of the English terms disciple, discipling, and discipleship. Is it possible to be a *disciple* without being on the road of discipleship? Is *discipling* different than *discipleship*?

5. Disciples as Converts in the Process of Discipleship

Still others suggest that a disciple is the true believer who enters the life of discipleship at the time of conversion. This model stresses that discipleship is vitally linked to conversion as the natural result. Discipleship is not a second step in the Christian life, but rather is synonymous with the Christian life itself. At conversion one becomes a disciple of Jesus, and the process of growth as a Christian is called discipleship.

For Dietrich Bonheoffer, for one to speak of entrance into the Christian life without recognizing the fact that it also means entrance into the life of discipleship is to cheapen the grace of God: "Cheap grace is grace without discipleship, grace without the cross, grace without Jesus Christ, living and incarnate." [8]

> Discipleship is not a second step in the Christian life, but rather is synonymous with the Christian life itself.

This model of discipleship emphasizes that as Jesus called men and women to Him, and as He sent His disciples out to make other disciples, He was calling men and women into a saving relationship with himself which would make a difference in the new disciple's life. Therefore, Jesus' purpose in the Great Commission included both conversion and growth; i.e., "making disciples" meant that one became a disciple at the moment of conversion and that growth in discipleship was the natural result of the new disciple's life. This is a life-long process.

II. Reconciling various aspects of discipleship in the New Testament [9]

For the discipleship ministry in the local church to reflect a more biblical focus we need to reconcile...

1. The call of grace by Jesus to discipleship and its strong demands

Jesus called by grace all that wanted to be his disciples, but as Master he established the conditions that they would need to meet with the help of the grace of God.

2. The ministry of Jesus to the multitudes and his ministry to his disciples

Overall, Jesus' discipleship teaching that was directed to the crowds dealt with the act of becoming a disciple (evangelism), whereas teaching directed to the disciples dealt with growth in discipleship (Christian growth).

3. The general passages on discipleship with the role of the Twelve

The Twelve—the closest followers of Jesus and in whom he dedicated the greater part of his time to train them— were both his disciples and apostles of the church. While in the gospels the Twelve are referred to as disciples, in Acts they are called apostles, emphasizing their function as leaders of the primitive church.

4. The profile of the disciples in the gospels and its references in Acts and the absence of the term "disciple" in the epistles

In the gospels and in Acts, "disciple" was the common designation of a believer in the primitive church. The book of Acts also helps us see the transitions that took place in discipleship terminology, since the word "disciple" does not occur at all in the epistles. Instead, other terms, such as brothers/sisters, saints, believers, and Christians came to be the prominent terms used to designate followers of Jesus. Although the term disciple does not occur in the epistles, the book of Acts allows us to see that at the same basic historical period as the writing of the epistles the terminology and concept of discipleship flourished.

III. Some key definitions [10]

1. Disciple, in general and specifically

In the general sense, we may define a disciple as a committed follower of a great master. The general sense of the term has two common applications: 1) It was used to distinguish the disciple from the teacher (Mt 10:24-25; Lk 6:40). 2) It was also used to designate the followers of a great leader or movement.

In the specific sense, a disciple of Jesus is one who has come to Jesus for eternal life, has claimed Jesus as Savior and God, and has embarked upon the life of following Jesus. A disciple is someone who is being transformed into the likeness of the Master in His way of living and carrying out His mission in his/her life.

2. Discipleship and Discipling

> Discipleship is the ongoing process of growth as a disciple.

The terms "discipleship" and "discipling," are English words derived, obviously, from disciple. The nearest equivalent to these expressions in the New Testament is the verbal form (mayhtenv), "make or become disciples," which occurs only four times (Mt 13:52; 27:57; 28:19; Acts 14:21). In common usage, "discipleship" and "discipling" today relate to the ongoing life of the disciple. "Discipleship" is the ongoing process of growth as a disciple. "Discipling" implies the responsibility of disciples helping one another grow as disciples (not just the new disciples).

Therefore, when we speak of Christian discipleship and discipling we are speaking of what it means to grow as a Christian in every area of life. Since "disciple" is a common referent for "Christian," discipleship and discipling imply the process of becoming like Jesus Christ. Discipleship and discipling mean living a fully human life in this world in union with Jesus Christ and growing in conformity to His image.

But when Jesus says that "a disciple is not above his teacher, but everyone when fully trained, will be like his teacher" (Luke 6:40), he enunciates a principle common to all master-disciple relationships: a disciple is involved in a natural process which will bring him or her to be like the master.

This principle is central to biblical discipleship: in this life a disciple is always in a discipleship process, the process of becoming like the Master, Jesus. Each disciple also has the responsibility to be involved in helping other disciples grow, i.e., discipling. Whether it be through the local discipleship ministry or through any of the other ministries of the church.

IV. Indispensable and Biblical elements for the local discipleship ministry

> Each disciple also has the responsibility to be involved in helping other disciples grow.

We should develop a discipleship ministry that is...

1. **Intentional**: on purpose, focused, organized, and structured, with its adjustments on the way, open to change.
2. **Interpersonal**: based on growing in intimacy in our personal relationship together in our vital relationship with Christ, being accountable to others. Ministering and challenging each other to greater commitment and involvement in compassionate service.
3. **Intergenerational**: geared towards persons of all ages (children, young people and adults) and in the family.
4. **Interminable**: life-long, guiding us through the different stages and situations in life. Discipleship should aim at our growth and advancement in our walk together with Christ, guiding us towards our maturity and service to others.
5. **Integral**: looking to meet all the different types of needs of the disciples.
6. **Intertwined**: within all of the community of faith, a group process.
7. **Integrative**: focusing all the ministries of the church to contribute with their unique resources to make disciples together.

> Intentional
> Interpersonal
> Intergenerational
> Interminable
> Integral
> Intertwined
> Integrative

Conclusion

To be disciples of Jesus is to enter into an intimate and growing relationship with the Master that guides us to be like Him in everything. So that during all our life we can grow in our relationship with Him to the point that we can, as a church, love as He loved, making others His disciples. This process begins at their conversion and continues through their constant participation in the mission of Christ through the church.

Integration Activity

1. Think of a symbol or metaphor that describes what a disciple of Jesus is.
2. Get together once again in the five small groups and prepare a sketch of about five minutes that shows, in a creative way, what is Christian discipleship.
3. Memorize the key Bible verse in Luke 6:40.

Focusing...

A study of the word Disciple(s) in the Gospels and in Acts

The word disciple, in singular form, appears in the gospels and in Acts, a total of 25 times in comparison to 235 times in the plural form, disciples. When the word disciple appears in the singular it usually is found in sayings about discipleship itself, what the disciple should be; in other words, it describes the type of relationship that should exist between the teacher and the disciple and the cost or requirements of a disciple. When the word disciples is used in plural, it normally describes what disciples do or have done, or is used as a direct reference to the disciples of Jesus.

Choose references of one of the Gospels or Acts below. Study these references and make a list of some of the characteristics of the disciples in that book.

The word "disciple(s)"		
In Matthew it appears 68 times	**In Mark appears 45 times**	**In Luke appears 33 times**
5:1; 8:23; 9:19; 10:1; 11:1; 12:49; 13:36; 14:19; 15:33, 36, 16:13, 21, 24; 17:6, 10, 19; 19:25; 20:17; 21:6, 20; 24:1, 3; 26:1, 8, 17, 19, 26, 35, 40, 56; 28:7, 8, 16, 19.	2:16, 18; 3:7, 9; 4:34; 5:31; 6:1, 7 (the Twelve), 35, 41; 7:5, 17; 8:1, 4, 6, 27, 33-34; 9:14, 18, 28, 31; 10:10, 13, 23-24, 46; 11:1, 14; 12:43; 13:1; 14:12-14, 16, 32, 50; 16:7, 12 (two of them).	5:30, 33; 6: 13, 17, 20: 7:11; 8:9, 22; 9:1, 14, 16, 18, 40, 54; 10:23; 11:1; 12:1, 22; 16:1; 17:1, 22; 18:15; 19:29, 37, 39; 20:45; 22:11, 39, 45; 24:36 (through them).

In John it appears 63 times	**In Acts it appears 26 times**
1:35, 37; 2:2, 11-12, 17, 22; 3:22; 4:27, 31, 33; 6:3, 8, 11-12, 60-61, 66; 7:3; 8:31; 9:2; 11:7-8, 12; 12:16; 13:5, 22-23, 35; 15:8; 16:17, 29; 18:1-2, 17, 19, 25; 20:10, 18-20, 25-26, 30; 21:1-2, 4, 8, 12, 14.	6:1-2, 7; 9:1, 19, 25-26, 38; 11:26, 29; 13:52; 14:20-22, 28; 15:10; 18:23, 27; 19:1-2, 9, 30; 20:1, 7, 30; 21:4, 16.

The characteristics of a disciple of Jesus in _____ are:

1. _____ 6. _____

2. _____ 7. _____

3. _____ 8. _____

4. _____ 9. _____

5. _____ 10. _____

Lesson 2

Biblical foundations for discipleship

General Objective

Train the trainers so they can sustain the discipleship ministry on solid biblical foundations, especially those of the New Testament.

Lesson Summary

- Some Old Testament foundations of discipleship.
- What does the New Testament say about discipleship?
- The Great Commission in Matthew.
- Jesus and discipleship.
- Discipleship in the Gospels.
- The primitive church in Acts and discipleship.
- Paul and the expansion of discipleship in other contexts.

Key verse to memorize

"Then he called the crowd to him along with his disciples and said: "If anyone would come after me, he must deny himself and take up his cross and follow me." (Mark 8:34; Galatians 2:20; Luke 14:27, NIV).

Group Exercise

Initial questions: Why are the biblical foundations of discipleship important in the church? What relationship should there be between the biblical foundations of discipleship and the discipleship ministry in the local church?

Introduction

Christian discipleship has its roots in the Old Testament but some of its principles continue into the New Testament and others do not. Some general Old Testament foundations for discipleship in the New Testament are: [1]

• The intimate discipleship relationship between God and his people reflected in the covenants (Leviticus 26:12).

- God expected his people to follow and walk with Him, loving him with all their heart and soul (Deuteronomy 10:12-13; 13:1-4; 1 Kings 18:21).
- There are some discipleship relationships in the Old Testament: Moses and Caleb; Elijah and Elisha; Jeremiah and Baruch.

Bill Hull emphasizes: "A recommitment to Christ's clear commands is the first order of business. The upgrading starts with establishment of the biblical foundations of the product... Disciple making should be installed at the heart of the church, and the commanded product of the church is a fruit-bearing believer called a disciple. Christ's command to His church to make disciples provides the scriptural mandate." [2]

The product that Jesus requires from the church is a person called a disciple.

I. What does the New Testament say about discipleship?

The word discipleship does not appear in the New Testament. Yet, *mathetes*, disciple and disciples, is found 262 times in the Gospels and in Acts. The word "disciple" does not appear in the rest of the New Testament literature. [3]

Christian discipleship...

- is what we are as followers of Jesus.
- is a life-style. What Jesus teaches is a way of life.
- has to do with a learning relationship between a student and his master. [4]

Christian discipleship is to BE and MAKE DISCIPLES in ... JESUS' style.

What is the mandate of the Great Commission?

While you are going, make disciples.

Group Exercise

Share a brief reflection about the cost of discipleship presented by Jesus in Luke 14:25-33. You can use the *Focusing* sheet at the end of this lesson.

1. Bearing the cross and the way of the cross

To "bear the cross" means to carry, daily, the instrument for our own execution. The people who died on a cross were condemned because of concrete decisions that they had made in their lives and because of the direction they had chosen in their commitments... the cross was the destiny of a life that was freely and voluntarily chosen. To take up the cross is a lifestyle that is *committed to what God wants to do in the world and with the values of the Kingdom*. The cross is a symbol of suffering and death. It is suffering for the cause of Christ to the point of being willing to die.

2. Discipleship is a complete and holistic surrender

To follow Jesus, a full surrender is required: denying oneself (Matthew 16:24), and giving to God one's family and everything one possesses (Luke 14:26, 33).

The fundamental characteristic that identifies a disciple of Jesus is that he/she is a "follower" (*akoloutheo*). They follow His steps, instructions, strategies, the ways and destiny (mission) of their Master, Jesus.

But we are not only called to be holistic disciples, but also to **make** such disciples. [5]

II. The Great Commission in Matthew

"Then Jesus came to them and said, "All authority in heaven and on earth has been given to me. Therefore go and make disciples of all nations, baptizing them in the name of the Father and of the Son and of the Holy Spirit, and teaching them to obey everything I have commanded you. And surely I am with you always, to the very end of the age." (Matthew 28:18-20, NIV)

There are three important elements of this commission to Jesus' disciples: [6]

- **The declaration of his authority:** "All authority in heaven and earth has been given to me".
- **The mandate to make disciples:** "...go (while you are going), make disciples of all nations, baptizing them in the name of the Father and the Son and the Holy Spirit, and teaching them to obey everything (all) I have commanded you".
- **The promise of his presence:** "And surely I am with you always (all the days), to the very end of the age."

Making disciples is the heart of the mission of the church.

The imperative —the mandate— of the great commission is to "make disciples".

Of whom? Of all nations.

How? Baptizing them...teaching them to obey everything I have commanded you... (Matthew 28:19).

"When we obey Christ's commission, two good things happen: we create healthy Christians; healthy Christians reproduce, and the body grows, and then multiplies, and the world is evangelized. [7]

Discipleship was so obvious to the first Christians that in the writings of the apostolic fathers there is no mention of the Great Commission. Yet, this was not an obstacle for carrying out the mission. [8]

III. Jesus and discipleship

The training style that Jesus utilized during his ministry was discipleship.

One of those days Jesus went out to a mountainside to pray, and spent the night praying to God. When morning came, he called his disciples to him and chose twelve of them, whom he also designated apostles. (Luke 6:12-13, NIV).

When Jesus began his ministry he appeared in the religious scene of his times as one more of those teachers of Israel. Therefore, he surrounded himself with some followers to teach them by his example to live as he did. The word teacher (didáscalos) appears in the gospels 48 times. We also find the word "Rabbi" 15 times and in two occasions "Rabboni" referring to Jesus as teacher.

Making disciples needs to be understood in the light of what it meant in the Jewish context and in the times Jesus lived: Jewish proselytism, the Hellenistic academies and the rabbinical schools. Jesus borrows some elements of these groups of his times but he also modifies them radically. [9]

Jesus distinguished himself from the rest of the teachers (rabbis) of his times in FIVE ways:

Teachers in the times of Jesus	Jesus' discipleship style
• The disciples choose their teacher.	• The teacher choose his disciples (John 15:16).
• Discipleship was for a temporal season.	• Discipleship was to be life-long (Luke 9:62).
• Disciples were practically slaves of their teacher.	• Jesus called his disciples friends (John 15:15).
• Only adult men were disciples.	• Jesus had disciples among children, women, young people and men (Mark 10:14, Luke 8:3).
• The disciples of a famous teacher received fame and social prestige.	• The disciples of Jesus are called to assume a cost, suffer and be willing to die (Matthew 5:11).

The central message of the Master

After this, Jesus traveled about from one town and village to another, proclaiming the good news of the kingdom of God. The Twelve were with him, (Luke 8:1 NIV).

- The message of Jesus zeroed in on the proclamation of the Kingdom. It was a call to a radical commitment with the values of the Kingdom of God.
- This message—of the coming of the Kingdom— also became the central message of the ministry of his followers (Matthew 10:5-15).

Therefore, Jesus' discipleship... [10]

1. Arises from a radical call by Jesus to follow him and to be involved in his mission of being a part of and building the Kingdom of God (Matthew 9:9; Mark 10:21). To follow him is to obey him, that is, to incorporate in one's life-style the teachings and mission of the Master. "It is clear that mathetes (disciple) means much more than 'student or learner'; it means to be a follower, one that keeps (obeys) the instruction one has been given and it becomes one's rule of conduct". [11]

2. Jesus calls his disciples to be with Him. The Lord of the Kingdom requires obedience, dependency on Him, and more than just knowledge of Him. But the purpose behind being with Him is so that "the life of the Lord can invade the life of his followers. It is Jesus that now lives in the lives of his followers". [12]

3. The call to discipleship is radical because it is a call to repentance, **metancia**, a new mind, a new mindset. In the New Testament, it means "a total and holistic reorganization of the life and personality of the individual that includes a new ethic for one's behavior, a rejection of sin turning back to the justice of God. It is a discipleship that trains others intentionally to share not only their lives but with their lives they share His mission". [13]

The most important element that defines a disciple is the teachings

IV. Discipleship in the gospels

Group Exercise
Observe and share the different characteristics of the teaching of Jesus in the following passages: Matthew 4:23; 11:1; Mark 6:1-2; 34; Luke 4:31-32; 8:9-10.

The most important element that defines a disciple is the teachings of Jesus. He was the maker of disciples; Jesus was addressing the disciples when he proclaimed the Great Commission.

In the gospels, "...to make disciples is not simply to lead men and women to follow Jesus, but also to train them so they can become channels of his grace. The promise of transforming Simon, Andrew and James into fishers of persons (Matthew 4:19; Mark 1:17) made implicit the continuation of the mission of Jesus through the life and ministry of his disciples, and through those that would become disciples through their ministry". [14] For this reason it was indispensable that the disciples stay close to the Master.

Profile of a disciple of Jesus the four gospels: [15]

Gospel	Image of a disciple	Biblical Passages
Matthew	Disciples who understand and obey the teachings of Jesus.	Matthew 12:49-50, 13:51, 16:12, 17:13.
Mark	Disciples as servants.	Mark 9:33-37, 10:35-45.
Luke	Disciples on the costly road of discipleship.	Luke 9:57-62, 18:24-30.
John	Disciples who believe and are marked by Jesus.	John 6:67, 70, 13:18, 15:16, 19. Three marks of disciples: they stay in the Word, 8:31-32; love one another, 13:34-35; and give fruits, 15:1-8.

V. The primitive church and discipleship in Acts

The apostles in the primitive church were characterized by following the example of their Master: making disciples.

And the word of God increased; and the number of the disciples multiplied in Jerusalem greatly; and a great company of the priests were obedient to the faith. (Acts 6:7 NIV)

Also in Acts the word disciple, *mathetes*, is used but it includes those that did not know Jesus directly, but were the result of the ministry of the first disciples and apostles (Acts 14:21-24).[16]

The apostles, before the great need of the people, maintained their ministry focused on prayer and the Word (Acts 6:2-4).

Two important characteristics of the disciples in Acts:
- As faithful disciples of Christ they were willing to suffer for the cause (9:1-2).
- They shared their material resources with their needy brothers and sisters (11:29-30).

VI. Paul and the expansion of discipleship in other contexts

Saul, after his conversion, was incorporated into the group of local disciples in Damascus (Acts 9:19). Later on, another disciple (Barnabas) went to Tarsus to find Saul and bring him to the church in Antioch (Acts 11:25-26).

Saul, who became Paul, also carried out his ministry making disciples. Read Acts 14:21-22a; 18:23, 27; 20:1-2, 7; 21:4-6, 16.

Paul continued the tradition of making disciples through his life and ministry, but he adds a new meaning to discipleship, using other words to describe a disciple without utilizing the word disciple in his writings. In this he is similar to us today, since most of us are in non-Jewish settings.

"Paul does not 'call' disciples like Jesus. Rather he presents himself as a mediating model of discipleship, and not as a substitute of the Master: *'Be ye followers (imitators) of me, even as I also am of Christ'* (1 Corinthians 11:1, KJV); in his relationship with his disciples he prefers the figure of 'father' in relationship with his 'children'". [17]

Therefore, "the defining, though not exclusive, metaphor that shapes Paul's understanding of the goal and the process of disciple making is spiritual parenting". [18] The Christian life is described in various passages of the New Testament as growing from spiritual infancy to maturity. The new believer is a spiritual babe, who eventually grows in Christ. While this growth takes place, the believer is also assuming the responsibility of discipling others. [19]

Examples where Paul talks about discipleship without using the word disciple:
- Colossians 1:28-29: He works to present everyone perfect in Christ.
- 1 Corinthians 9:25: He challenges believers to enter the Christian race as athletes.
- 1 Corinthians 3:1-2; 14:20 Ephesians 4:13-14: Paul contrasts being mature with the abnormal condition of being infants in the faith, when they should be teachers.

For Paul, the goal of discipleship —that transformative process— is "to be conformed to the likeness of his Son" (Romans 8:29) or to "present everyone perfect in Christ" (Colossians 1:28).

Conclusion

In the primitive church and in the New Testament, there is an intimate relationship between evangelism and discipleship. The starting point and what saturated everything they did was discipleship.

It was well understood that the mission of the church was to make disciples, and the first Christians as disciples went out to share the gospel to make new disciples. In our days we have inverted the process: we disciple as a consequence of our evangelism. And it has cost us so much time and effort to incorporate discipleship in our evangelism!

For Paul, "the metaphor that defines and molds... the process of making disciples is that of a spiritual father."

GREG OGDEN

As we have seen, the emphasis in making disciples is not an isolated theme, but it permeates all of the New Testament:

- beginning with the constant use of the word "disciple" in the Gospels and in Acts,
- the emphasis of making disciples in the Great Commission,
- the ministry of Jesus focused on making disciples
- the different descriptions of a disciple in the Gospels,
- the ministry of the primitive church dedicated to making disciples, and
- in Paul's ministry he carried out making disciples of the gentiles in a new setting.

Paul describes his process of discipleship with the church in Thessalonica in his first letter to them (2:7b-8, 11-13a, NIV) in the following way:

...like a mother caring for her little children. We loved you so much that we were delighted to share with you not only the gospel of God but our lives as well, because you had become so dear to us... For you know that we dealt with each of you as a father deals with his own children, encouraging, comforting and urging you to live lives worthy of God, who calls you into his kingdom and glory. And we also thank God continually....

Integration Activity

1. Is discipleship an isolated theme in the New Testament that only refers to Jesus and his ministry?
2. What are some of the most outstanding and recurring discipleship principles in the New Testament?
3. How would you bring together, in practice, the discipleship focus of Jesus, the Gospels and Paul´s perspective?

Focusing...

Reflection on the cost of discipleship in Luke 14:25-33

"Large crowds were traveling with Jesus, and turning to them he said: 'If anyone comes to me and does not hate his father and mother, his wife and children, his brothers and sisters—yes, even his own life—he cannot be my disciple. And anyone who does not carry his cross and follow me cannot be my disciple.

Suppose one of you wants to build a tower. Will he not first sit down and estimate the cost to see if he has enough money to complete it? For if he lays the foundation and is not able to finish it, everyone who sees it will ridicule him, saying, 'This fellow began to build and was not able to finish.'

Or suppose a king is about to go to war against another king. Will he not first sit down and consider whether he is able with ten thousand men to oppose the one coming against him with twenty thousand? If he is not able, he will send a delegation while the other is still a long way off and will ask for terms of peace. In the same way, any of you who does not give up everything he has cannot be my disciple'" (NIV).

These guiding questions will help you reflect on the true cost of discipleship:

1. To whom is Jesus addressing these words according to verse 25?

_____

_____

_____

2. Which are the conditions that Jesus establishes for those that want to become his disciples according to verses 26-27?

_____

_____

_____

3. What do the two illustrations in verses 28-32 reveal about being disciples of Jesus?

_____

_____

_____

4. What other condition is required to be a disciple of Jesus as found in verse 33?

_____

_____

_____

5. How can these discipleship principles in Luke 14:25-33 be applied to the church today?

_____

_____

Lesson 3

Discipleship as Christian Spiritual formation

General Objective

Equip the trainers to center the process of discipleship of the local church in the constant spiritual formation of each disciple. That they may learn to nurture each other through the personal and collective spiritual disciplines and be committed to serve others.

Lesson Summary

- Spiritual formation is the consistent center of the discipleship process.
- Daily and faithfully cultivate your relationship with God together with others.
- Personal discipleship: knowing and using the spiritual disciplines.
- Group discipleship: learning and practicing the spiritual disciplines together.
- Discipleship saturated and guided by the Holy Spirit.

Key verse to memorize

"By this all men will know that you are my disciples, if you love one another… My prayer is not for them alone. I pray also for those who will believe in me through their message, that all of them may be one, Father, just as you are in me and I am in you. May they also be in us so that the world may believe that you have sent me" (John 13:35; 17:20-21, NIV).

Group Exercise

Each person share briefly how he/she met and gave their life to Christ and specify how they have grown spiritually throughout the years.

Introduction

The heart of Christian discipleship is the process of spiritual formation of the disciple within the community of faith fulfilling its mission. More than just providing spiritual information, we need to involve each disciple, from the beginning, in a shared pilgrimage. In this walk, the disciples should be spiritually shaped and nurtured for their own development, so that down the road, they can teach others to feed themselves and make disciples of others.

Definition of spiritual formation: "the whole person in relationship with God, within the community of believers, growing in Christlikeness, reflected in a Spirit-directed, disciplined lifestyle, and demonstrated in redemptive action in our world." [1]

Three powerful enemies of spiritual formation in our days:

1. Superficiality: Richard Foster wrote in 1978: "Superficiality is the curse of our age. The doctrine of instant satisfaction is a primary spiritual problem. The desperate need today is not for a greater number of intelligent people, or gifted people, but for deep people. The classical Disciplines of the spiritual life call us to move from surface living to the depths"[2]

2. Lack of time, excessive busyness in so many insignificant activities and the rush in getting things done. We should seek the simplicity of life.
3. Inconsistency or lack of discipline in our time with God. Discipline needs to become a priority for our life, to the point that it becomes a habit that helps us grow and be built-up constantly.

The spiritual formation of disciples should include…

> **Group Exercise**
> Share some metaphors, images or symbols that reflect what spiritual formation is for you.

I. Daily and faithfully cultivate your relationship with God together with others

The indispensable element in discipleship as a life-long process is cultivating our relationship with Christ through the spiritual disciplines. We need to be aware of the spiritual disciplines and experience them as means of grace to learn how to nurture ourselves spiritually. This will guide us toward maturity and to a greater commitment to the mission of God in the world through the church.

Although there is an important personal dimension in our relationship with Christ that we need to cultivate, at the same time, we should have a spiritual mentor or a small group that is committed to our ongoing growth. In this way we can be accountable to others for our spiritual progress and share and receive help in our personal struggles.

Jesus called those that would become his disciples telling them:

"**Come ye after me,** and I will make you to become fishers of men." (Mark 1:17, KJV)

"As Jesus went on from there, he saw a man named Matthew sitting at the tax collector's booth. '**Follow me,**' he told him, and Matthew got up and followed him." (Matthew 9:9, NIV)

"**Come to me**, all you who are weary and burdened, and I will give you rest." (Matthew 11:28, NIV)

The constant call of Jesus to us… is not initially to a task,…but rather… to himself.

The constant call of Jesus to us who are already his disciples —as it was from the beginning—is not initially to a task, nor to a ministry, nor to a job, but rather his call is always, in first place, to himself. It is a call to have an intimate, constant and permanent relationship with Him. This is the fundamental issue of our mission, where mission begins.

This permanent encounter with Him will lead us to worship and obey Him in everything. In the process we become more like Him in our character, in our thoughts, in our attitudes, in what we feel, in our motivations, in our perspectives, in what we do and in what we dedicate our lives to. We make his mission and his life-style ours. A transfer of His life to our life begins and the transformation of our being to His image, so that now he can live His life through our life.

> **Group Exercise**
> Share how you nurture yourself spiritually every day. What methods or forms, common and unusual, do you use for your constant spiritual growth?

II. Personal discipleship: knowing and using the spiritual disciplines

As I refer to personal discipleship I want to underscore the importance of discipline, motivation and self-initiative. We need to live daily experiencing the grace of God through the spiritual disciplines in our personal encounter as an indispensable priority.

"Discipline in the spiritual life is the concentrated effort of creating the space and time where God can become our Master and where we can freely respond to the direction of God." [3]

Habits we should practice in the discipleship process as we guide others:

1. Focus the discipleship of others on guiding them to learn to nurture themselves and not only to depend solely on the nurture of others. This requires instruction, modeling, and being accompanied in the Christian life by one or more people who are more mature in their faith.

2. Guide the persons to establish a "rule of life," maybe monthly or yearly, and to be committed to carrying it out daily for their constant development in the faith. We need structure and support from others for our spiritual formation.

   This rule of life refers to a plan of how we are going to spend time alone with God, what materials we will systematically study and which biblical passages we will utilize—the format of our intimate time with God—and which activities we will engage in, whether it be by ourselves or with other Christians to continue in our spiritual renewal (although it is open to change along the way, view the Focusing exercise at the end of this lesson).

3. Be mutually accountable regarding our spiritual growth and/or the obstacles we face. In this process it is crucial we share what we've learned during our daily personal devotions.

III. Group discipleship: learning and practicing the spiritual disciplines together

Generally speaking, spiritual disciplines are learned and developed more effectively in small groups. We have to ask ourselves, according to the Bible: What does each of the spiritual disciplines consist of? How can they be taught? And how does one develop them? We will go on to briefly describe some of the spiritual disciplines:

- **Prayer**: Communication and communion with God. Through prayer, we communicate to God what is in our hearts, not because he does not already know what is there but because it pleases him that we empty ourselves in his presence as an act of faith and total dependency on Him. We also pray to have fellowship and communion with God, and in that way we can hear his voice.

- **Reading, studying and meditating on Scriptures**: The most complete and authoritative source for our spiritual development is the Bible, the written Word of God. It is the book that shows us who God is, who is his Son—our Master and the savior of the world—and his redemptive purposes for our lives. Scriptures provide the spiritual food that our souls longs for. That is why we should learn to read, interpret, study and apply it constantly to our personal lives and as members of the Body of Christ (This is called inductive Bible study).

- **Fasting:** It is a spiritual exercise in which we abstain from food to focus on prayer, communion and enjoying God in our lives. More than anything else, fasting is a source of personal spiritual renewal and renewal as a community of faith. When we fast, we take part in the spiritual banquet that God has laid before us, free from internal and external distractions, for our edification and motivation for committed service.

- **Spiritual Reading:** It is the reading of devotional writers who share their perspectives and lessons learned so we can develop a more intimate relationship with God. There are some classic and contemporary books that, when read and studied together, permits the Spirit to strengthen and guide us in our walk with Christ, as He did with these earlier Christians.

- **Contemplation:** It is to meditate, focused on nature, life and even in our inner being to discover the mighty hand of God. Meditation and contemplation naturally go together.

...guiding them to learn to nurture themselves and not only to depend solely on the nurture of others

It is a way of stopping in the midst of the daily busyness of life and focusing ourselves on God. Contemplation is also a powerful means of prayer.

- **Worship:** It is a means of centering ourselves in God. We exalt and honor him, recognizing who He is and His powerful works. True worship is as much an act as it is a life-style of gratitude and availability to God. Collective worship is a powerful means to unite us, edify us through singing, testimonies and the proclamation or preaching of the Word. It is in worship, centered in God, that we understand and are compelled to the fulfillment of our mission as the church in the world.

- **The sacraments:** As Wesleyan Christians we consider the sacraments of Baptism and the Lord's Supper as two powerful means of grace instituted by Christ for our permanent spiritual growth. In other words, these two sacraments are means by which the grace of God is distributed to us for our collective spiritual strength and commitment.

To use our spiritual formation as a means to grow as disciples of Jesus it is very important that we ask ourselves: How can we guide our discipleship groups so that the spiritual disciplines can become central to its dynamic?

We need to remind ourselves that our spiritual formation is not an end in itself; it should always move us to serve others, that is, help us as disciples in carrying out our mission of reaching and discipling others.

"Constant spiritual growth would be a frustrating impossibility if it were not for... the Holy Spirit."

ROBERTO SUDERMAN

IV. Discipleship saturated and guided by the Spirit [4]

Christian discipleship and our constant spiritual growth would be a frustrating impossibility if it were not for the reality and activity of the Holy Spirit. The beginning, and the vitality and continuity of our spiritual life, is directly dependant on the penetrating work of the Holy Spirit as it opens us up to His movement in and through us.

Although the Bible reminds us that the Holy Spirit was active in the life and ministry of Jesus (see Luke 1:35, 67; 2:25-27; 3:22; 4:1, 14, 18), it also indicates that believers received a special power when Jesus finished his ministry and returned to the Father (Matthew 18:19-20; John 16:7; 20:22; Acts. 2:1-12; Galatians 5). This special presence of the Spirit in His disciples suggests that he/she is a carrier and spokesperson of a special "spirituality" in this world (Galatians 5:5-6).

In this way discipleship and spirituality are inseparable. "Only when we understand that our spirituality most clearly manifests itself in the 'follow after me' of our Master can we affirm that discipleship and Christian spirituality do not contradict each other. The endeavor of edifying lives under the power of the Spirit that reflect Jesus' call to take up our cross and follow him in our lives, is our call to discipleship, and at the same time, our commitment to be authentically spiritual persons." [5]

Conclusion

As faithful disciples of Jesus, we become the project and method of God.

E. M Bounds (1835-1913), a Methodist minister, in his book Power Through Prayer declares:

"We are constantly on a stretch, if not on a strain, to devise new methods, new plans, new organizations to advance the Church and secure enlargement and efficiency for the gospel. This trend of the day has a tendency to lose sight of the man or sink the man in the plan or organization. God's plan is to make much of the man, far more of him than of anything else. Men [and women] are God's method. The Church is looking for better methods; God is looking for better men [and women]...What the Church needs today is not more machinery or better, not new organizations or more and novel methods, but men [and women] whom

the Holy Ghost can use—men [and women] of prayer, men [and women] mighty in prayer. The Holy Ghost does not flow through methods, but through men [and women]. He does not come on machinery, but on men [and women]. He does not anoint plans, but men [and women] — men [and women] of prayer." [6]

We minister from who we are, who we have become as we are formed in Christ, and who we continue being in our walk with Him.

We grow as we participate in the means of grace personally and collectively. In this case, it would be to recover our Wesleyan heritage: prayer, reading and studying Scriptures and the sacraments. Let us rediscover these elements and make them available to our brothers and sisters and non-Christians as a vital part of our continual discipleship.

Integration Activity

1. Present some of your prayer requests regarding your spiritual development so that you can pray one for another.
2. What practical measures can you take so you can be open to the work of the Holy Spirit in the discipleship group?

"Men [and women] are the method of God".

E. M. BOUNDS

Focusing...

Discipline in the spiritual life, creating and carrying out a Rule of life*

As disciples of Jesus we need structure and support for our spiritual growth. A Rule of Life is a spiritual plan that we prepare so we can nurture ourselves with the spiritual food that will take us to a more intimate relationship with Christ, our Master. One needs to make significant decisions to utilize the spiritual disciplines for our growth in holiness.

It is important to consider the following to create a Rule of Life that fits you:

- Observe where you find yourself spiritually at the present. What type of relationship with Christ do you have? In what areas do you need to go deeper?
- To which spiritual disciplines are you attracted the most and why? Maybe your personality is more at ease practicing these disciplines.
- To which spiritual disciplines are you not attracted and may even repulse you? Pray about this. Maybe your negative reaction reflects that you are resisting to take care of a part of your life that needs healing.
- Be open to the areas of your life where possibly God wants to stretch you and make you grow. What area or areas of your life are you committed to develop as your priority?
- Analyze your personal circumstances in the present to determine how much time and in what time frames you can schedule for your constant spiritual growth.
- Choose someone which you trust to share your Rule of Life with and to whom you will be accountable to for your progress; it could be a spiritual formation group.

Take a sheet of paper and draw a vertical line that divides the sheet in half. Then approximately two-thirds down into the sheet draw a horizontal line. You would have four quadrants as shown below. You will write from on the two top boxes from left to right the words "daily" and "weekly". In the two boxes below from left to right you will write the words "monthly" and "yearly" (see example below).

Write in each one of the quadrants what you are already doing for your spiritual growth in each time frame and how you can improve these. Then include what you feel God wants you to add. You should consider practices that will help you worship God, grow personally and serve others.

Daily	Weekly
Monthly	Yearly

* Marjorie J. Thompson, Soul Feast, Louisville, KY: Westminster John Knox Press, 1995: 137-146.

Lesson 4

Discipleship as a means of multiplication and small groups

General Objective

Guide the trainers to embrace the fact that discipleship is the biblical method of multiplication, and that ministering in small groups is an effective means for the continual growth and multiplication of disciples and disciplers.

Lesson Summary

- Multiplication is why the church exists.
- The mandate of making disciples is multiplication based on quality.
- Multiplication focuses us on the future.
- Small groups can be an effective means of multiplication.
- Different group size.
- Small group dynamics.

Key verse to memorize

"And the word of God increased; and the number of the disciples multiplied in Jerusalem greatly; and a great company of the priests were obedient to the faith." (Acts 6:7, KJV).

Group Exercise

Share what multiplication means to you in the light of the ministry of the church.

Introduction

The church exists to multiply itself. This was the model of Christ as he had disciples that accompanied him and in whom he focused his ministry. It was precisely to make disciples that he sent his followers to do in the Great Commission: which is an urgent call to multiplication of disciples. This was the same emphasis of the first church under the direction and the power of the Holy Spirit. Multiplication was the pattern we see in Paul's missionary ministry through local gentile churches. The result of this multiplication is the vision John received of heaven (Revelation 7:9-17).

Therefore, we cannot talk about discipleship without talking about multiplication. "Discipleship training is the spiritual work of developing spiritual maturity and spiritual reproductiveness in the life of a Christian...a multiplier is a disciple who is training his spiritual children to reproduce themselves." [1]

I. Multiplication is why the church exists

"The people of God were created to be a community in whose midst authentic followers of the Lord would be multiplied. They would be a community that expresses an authentic life, the reality of the Kingdom of the Kyrios (Lord)." [2] Men and women who would live, experience, and propagate that culture to others.

...we cannot talk about discipleship without talking about multiplication.

One is impacted and impressed by the multiplication dynamic of the church in the first centuries, considering that before Pentecost the Christian church had only a few hundred believers. Paul mentions 500 believers in 1 Corinthians 15:6.

"Probably the Christian community within three decades had multiplied four hundredfold, which represents an annual increase of 22 percent for more than a generation, and the rate of growth continued remarkably high for 300 years.

By the beginning of the fourth century, when Constantine was converted to Christianity, the number of disciples may have reached 10 or 12 million; roughly a tenth of the total population of the Roman Empire…the early church grew by evangelistic multiplication as witnesses of Christ reproduced their life-style in the lives of those about them." [3]

II. The mandate of making disciples is multiplication based on quality

"Only healthy disciples reproduce. If the church fails to make disciples, it fails to multiply. If the church fails to multiply, it fails. The command was not 'make converts' or 'make Christians' or 'make church members'…The commission's command to make disciples is the imperative to produce a quality product. The church must produce people who reproduce themselves; any other kind of Christian is spiritually sterile." [4]

"Each Christian must see themselves as the link to the next generation."

WILLIAM BARCLAY

Reproduction is different from multiplication. The reproduction of a disciple is marvelous, but this is nothing more than spiritual addition. In theory a disciple can guide many to Christ, but if none of those converts pass it on, there is reproduction but not multiplication. [5]

Although multiplication focuses on large amounts of people, it will only take place if one dedicates him/herself to a few with a vision of reproduction for various generations. "Jesus had enough vision to think small" [6] : he dedicated himself to a few. "The irony is that in our attempt to reach the masses through massive means we have failed to train people the masses could emulate. We often perpetuate superficiality by casting a wider net, without the commensurate depth." [7]

When Jesus focused on a few he did not reflect his indifference for multitudes, rather he wants us to see that he had another way of reaching them, not through massive means but through persons filled with Him, by the quality of life of his followers.

III. Multiplication focuses us towards the future

The emphasis on multiplication permits us to look beyond the past and the present of the church and it projects us into the future, allowing us to leave a legacy behind for the new generations.

There are at least four principles of multiplication in 2 Timothy 2:2: "And the things you have heard me say in the presence of many witnesses entrust to reliable men who will also be qualified to teach others" (NIV).

1. Multiplication requires that the baton be passed on various times. Here four generations are mentioned: Paul, Timothy, reliable men, and others.
2. Multiplication requires that those who have received the Gospel must pass it on.
3. Multiplication requires passing the baton to reliable persons.
4. Multiplication requires passing the baton to qualified people. Multiplication needs to be carried out by persons with a Christlike character, who have gifts and skills to share the Gospel and motivate that it be passed on to the next generation. [8]

William Barclay used to say that "each Christian must see themselves as the link to the next generation… [we must] return to small, reproducible, long-term relationships as the means of transmission of the Gospel from one generation to the next." [9]

Christian Schwarz reminds us that "the principle of multiplication applies to all the areas of church life: Just as the true fruit of an apple tree is not an apple, but another tree; the true fruit of a small group is not a new Christian, but another group; the true fruit of a church is not a new group but a new church; the true fruit of a leader is not a follower, but a new leaders; the true fruit of an evangelist is not a convert but new evangelists." [10]

IV. Small groups can be an effective means of multiplication

Group Exercise

How has your experience been with small groups in the church? What kind of spiritual growth and relationships have you had with group members?

Discipleship led by Jesus, by the primitive church and by Paul was a small group movement. As was mentioned earlier, it is significant that the word "disciple", in its singular form, appears in the Gospels and Acts, only 25 times in comparison with 235 times "disciples", in the plural form.

> Discipleship led by Jesus, by the primitive church and by Paul was a small group movement.

"From the beginning Jesus brings together a "team" of disciples so they can function as a group...At times one or another disciple surpasses the others, but they are always in company of the group that surrounds them. The Gospels present a group dynamic of the disciples in spite of the temporal ruptures and occasional rivalry (they go together, they have common questions, they stay close together)." [11]

Since discipleship is centered on relationships, small groups can be a type of seed bed to cultivate first our vital relationship with Christ, and then our relationships with each other as part of our testimony and life. We also establish intimate relationships and friendships as we are discipled together.

"Jesus mandated disciplemaking, something that always happens within three relational dynamics—large groups, small groups, and life to life [one-on-one]...each one has strengths and limitations...the intentional disciplemaking community benefits by learning when and how to use each one [group] most effectively...for maximum impact, it's important to understand and play with all three." [12]

An important fact from the history of the Church:

> "It was in 323, almost three hundred years after the birth of the church, that Christians first met in something we now call a 'church building'... For all three hundred years before that, the church met in living rooms! Indeed, during the first three centuries of church growth, leaders typically ministered without large-group dynamics. Persecution and lack of mega facilities may partially explain why. However, when Christianity became a popular national religion under Roman emperor Constantine in the fourth century, large groups became the ministry norm." [13]

V. Different group size

Large Groups

The greatest weakness of the large group is that it only serves to tell people what they should believe and why. This is a first and important step in disciple making, but only a start. [14] The big group or event can be used effectively to inspire, inform and motivate. We should realize that few can direct large groups well.

Small Groups

Small groups of four to twelve people typically move toward a more intimate community dynamic, one where members feel enough security and trust to share the dreams, fears, and concerns that they could never reveal in a larger group. Because it is harder to hide in a small group, a sense of ownership and responsibility to each other develops as well. [15] Today, small groups are widely used in many quarters.

One on one

This is a personal, mentoring relationship in which one person "empowers another by sharing God-given resources… Mentoring is a great way to rejuvenate your passion for Christ and your sense of mission while encouraging someone else to grow in the same direction." [16]

Up to now, in many places, discipleship has been pretty much focused on a one-on-one relationship; yet, there are some limitations in this dynamic that we should recognize to see how we can compensate for these shortcomings : [17]

1. The discipler carries all the responsibility for the spiritual welfare of the new disciple.
2. A hierarchical relationship is usually set up that tends to result in dependency and lack of mutuality in the discipleship process.
3. This type of relationship limits interchange or dialogue since a mature Christian is discipling a new believer.
4. The new disciple is exposed to the influence of just one perspective, and in this way he/she receives the strengths and weakness of the discipler.
5. This model usually does not reproduce. Without a lot of thought, we have inadvertently held up a hierarchical, positional model that is nontransferable. As long as there is a sense that one person is over another by virtue of a superior spiritual authority, however that is measured, few people will see themselves as qualified to disciple others.

"a triad is the ideal size for a disciple-making group".

GREG OGDEN

However, there are three types of mentoring relationships in which the one-on-one method can be effective: as spiritual guide, coach and sponsor. [18]

Groups of three

Greg Ogden, pastor and discipler, after using for years small groups and the one on one method, affirms "a triad as the ideal size for a disciple-making group…the group of three appears to maximize the transformative dynamics in a discipleship relationship." [19]

Adding one more person to the one-on-one method makes discipleship energizing, joy-filled and reproductive, as there is a shift from…

1. the unnatural pressure to natural participation of the discipler.
2. a hierarchical [relationship] to a relational focus.
3. dialogue [between two persons] to a dynamic interchange.
4. limited input to the wisdom of the numbers.
5. addition to multiplication. [20]

The group of three provides: [21]
1. Multiplication or reproduction: empowering those who are discipled to disciple others.
2. Intimate Relationships: developing deep trust as the soil for life change.
3. Accountability: lovingly speaking truth into another's life.
4. Incorporation of the biblical message: covering the themes of Scripture sequentially to create a holistic picture of the Christian life.
5. Spiritual Disciplines: practicing the habits that lead to intimacy with Christ and service to others.

VI. Small group dynamics

Strategies for small groups

The group leader is the key person in the small group. "The quality of a small group is literally dependent on the qualifications of its leader [the aptitudes and spiritual life of its leader]. That is why it is so important that (a) only those persons who are spiritually gifted for this task be called as small group leaders, and (b) these Christians be well trained for their ministry. [22] We should pay attention to a leader's:

1. Spiritual life.
2. Skills to work in a group setting.
3. Constant training in all aspects of his/her life and ministry.
4. Commitment to the church and other leaders (loyalty).
5. Understanding of his/her place and contribution within the total ministry of the local church.
6. Need to be supervised and meet weekly or periodically with the other small group leaders.
7. Comprehension of the type of group he/she is leading, that is, the main focus of the group.
8. Work with a small team to train others.
9. Vision for multiplication, that this vision is caught and developed.

The quality of a small group is literally dependent on the qualifications of its leader

Four essential elements in small groups: care (fellowship), growth (be accountable), training (multiplication) and task (evangelism and service). Although in each group these elements may be present, "the task of every new small group must be to decide which of the four elements will represent the group's focus." [23] It is also important to decide how long the group will operate and the level of commitment expected from its participants.

Practical steps for the cell ministry (home groups) [24]

1. Make sure small group leaders are trained for their work.
2. Pay attention to the consistent application of the apprentice-leader principle.
3. Encourage a planned process of multiplication.
4. Have the courage to let some groups die.
5. Provide appropriate resources for the content development of the groups.
6. Make sure you have different types of groups.
7. Make the coaching of your group leaders your priority.
8. Monitor the effectiveness of your actions.

Conclusion

"The priority of our ministry should be to 'make disciples'…Our goal is not reduced to being disciples, but producing them; which necessarily implies that we become teachers (disciplers). We are teachers not because of the doctrine we transmit, rather by the new disciples we multiply. The only method to assure that the chain is not broken and that we continue with the work God has entrusted us is training trainers. Efficiency is not measured by what we do, but by what others do. The only path to multiply ourselves is forming others that in turn will train others as disciples of Jesus. It is not enough that we be disciples. It is not sufficient that we produce disciples. It is necessary that we train teachers (disciplers). It is not enough that we add our strengths: we have to multiply them." And the strategic use of small groups will help us in the process of multiplying disciples.

Integration Activity

1. What practical steps can be taken to imprint the vision of multiplication in the work of the church?
2. Which necessary steps can be taken to implement and develop the discipleship ministry using small groups in the local church as a means of development and multiplication?
3. Which group size (one on one, 4-12 persons, and triads) do you feel most comfortable with to grow as a disciple and develop future disciplers?

Focusing...

Multiplication Exercises

1. We begin with 12 disciples in six groups of twos and during a year each group wins one person each month, which are 12 per year. Then the same pattern is followed: the amount of disciples is divided into groups of twos so that each group reaches 12 during the year, How many disciples will there be in 10 years? Follow the example below and calculate for 10 years.

Year	Calculation	Total Amount of Disciples
1	12÷2 = 6 x 12	72
2	72÷2 = 36 x 12	432
3	432÷2 = 216 x 12	2,592
4		
5		
6		
7		
8		
9		
10		

2. An evangelist wins one person per day, how many would he have won in 16 years? (Addition) Versus a discipler who wins one per year and disciples him/her and duplicates him/herself each year for 16 years. How many disciples would have been trained at the end of this time? (Multiplication)

3. Someone has an option of either receiving a salary of US $10,000 per month, or begin making one cent the first day (0.01) but duplicating this amount each day for 30 days. Which salary would you choose?

Wesley's small groups

John Wesley used small groups in his ministry. He called them societies, classes, and bands. They guided new believers from conversion, to spiritual maturity and eventually to a point where they became effective leaders in the mission of the church.

Below is an example of the questions that Wesley used in his bands, which were more advanced groups, to go deeper in the persons' spiritual growth. The following are the five questions that everyone responded to in each meeting:

1. What known sins have you committed since our last meeting?
2. What temptations have you encountered?
3. How were you freed from them?
4. Have you thought, said or done anything that makes you doubt that you have sinned?
5. Do you have a secret that you would like to keep to yourself?

First the leader of the group answered these personal questions honestly before the group, and then the other group members shared their responses to the same set of questions. The purpose was to know their real spiritual struggles and needs without judging or condemning.

Personal or group exercises

Answer these five questions weekly for a month, whether it is in an intimate small group or writing the answers in your personal diary. How have you progressed in your spiritual life during this month? Is it worth it to continue with this practice?

Lesson 5
Discipleship for pastors

General Objective

Motavate the trainers to value the formative ministry of the pastor and the community of faith that focuses its vocation and local service in making disciples of all the persons in the church.

Lesson Summary

- The urgent need of pastors as makers of disciples.
- Discipleship in the New Testament required pastoral leadership.
- Discipleship in the New Testament is based on a balanced pastoral vocation in constant renewal.
- Discipleship in the New Testament included discipleship of pastors.
- Priorities of the disciple making pastor.
- The pastor as maker of a community of disciples.

Key verse to memorize

"Remember your leaders [pastors], who spoke the word of God to you. Consider the outcome of their way of life and imitate their faith.... Obey your leaders [pastors] and submit to their authority. They keep watch over you as men who must give an account. Obey them so that their work will be a joy, not a burden, for that would be of no advantage to you" (Hebrews 13:7, 17, NIV).

Introduction

One of the greatest and most urgent needs of the church and the world today are PASTORS.

A. Jesus saw the needy world, without God and salvation, as sheep without a shepherd (a pastor); and this awoke with in him compassion for them (Matthew 9:36).

B. The resurrected Christ enstrusted Peter three times with this command, on his way to his restoration, "Do you love me?,...feed (pastor) my sheep" (John 21:17).

C. Pastoral leadership is important in the discipleship ministry of the local church. Leroy Eims, in his book, *The Lost Art of Disciple Making* says:

"Every believer in Jesus Christ deserves the opportunity of personal nurture and development. Every new believer is expected to achieve his or her full potential for God. And most of them would if they had the opportunity, if **someone** would get the food within reach, if **someone** would give them the help they need, if **someone** would give them the training they should have, and if **someone** would care enough to suffer a little, sacrifice a little, and pray a lot." [1]

"The concepts and principles [of discipleship]...do not emerge from a philosophy of speedy growth and instant maturity. True growth takes time and tears

> **Group Exercise**
>
> Reflect on the following questions: At the present, do we really need pastors in the church or would it be better to let the lay leaders run the church without a pastor? What relation is there between discipleship and the pastoral ministry in the local church?

> "Every believer in Jesus Christ deserves the opportunity of personal nurture and development... And the pastor knew he was the key to this."
>
> LEROY EIMS

and love and patience. On the leader's [the pastor's] part, it takes faith to see people as God expects them to be and wants them to become. And it takes some knowledge to help get them there." [2]

The pastor "knew that unless he trained some spiritually qualified workers among the men and women of his congregation, many people would not get needed help in the initial stages of Christian growth (adequate follow-up) and would not develop into strong, robust disciples of Jesus Christ. And the pastor knew he was the key to this. The whole process had to begin with him…As the spiritual leader of these people; he had to lead the way." [3]

D. Although the need for pastors is urgent, God and the Church needs a certain type of pastors, that is to say,…

1. **a pastor-disciple that…**
   - consider his/her priority is to grow daily in an intimate and committed relationship with the Master.
   - have a spiritual mentor and/or are formed by other pastors.
   - participate in a small group for his or her spiritual growth as pastors.

2. **a pastor-discipler that…**
   - trains an intimate group of lay pastors and leaders (disciplers).
   - personally disciples other believers.

3. **a pastor-driven by discipleship to evangelize and do missions**
   - continual discipleship ministry (teaching and modeling).
   - ministering to others (service).

4. **a pastor-constructor of a community of disciples**
   - Conscientiously focuses discipleship as the model for pastoral ministry and for the local church.
   - Utilizes all of the pastoral functions: preaching, teaching, administration and pastoral care to shape a discipling congregation. Creates and provides the corporate atmosphere to grow together, in communion and fellowship as a community of faith.
   - Focuses all the ministries of the church: worship, communion, teaching, service, evangelism and the church's constant growth so they can all contribute to making disciples.
   - Involves all the different age groups in the church in discipleship, that is, discipleship among children, young people and adults.

I. **Discipleship in the New Testament did not happen spontaneously**

Discipleship in the New Testament did not happen spontaneously nor did it occur as a suggestion from some member of the church, it was propelled by leaders, the pastors of the flock.

To make disciples is the imperative of the Great Commission and the heart of the mission of the church. Discipleship became the training style of leader-pastors like Jesus, the apostles in the primitive church, Paul and others.

> Discipleship in the New Testament is based on a balanced pastoral vocation in constant renewal.

Group Exercise

As pastor or lay leader, Which of the following have been your obstacles in discipleship within the church?
- I was not discipled intentionally.
- I was not part of a church that had discipleship as its model for ministry.
- I was not trained in discipleship for the pastoral ministry or as a lay leader.
- I have operated for years with other paradigms for ministry (not discipleship).
- Discipleship has only been for new believers, so that we do not lose people, or only to learn more from the Bible.
- Other:

Group Exercise

How can lay leaders collaborate with pastors so that together they can develop an effective local discipleship ministry?

II. Discipleship in the New Testament is based on a balanced pastoral vocation in constant renewal

Today we need to recessitate the pastoral vocation. Ricardo Barbosa de Sousa, pastor and Brazilian theologian, writer of *Above All Guard your Heart* (*Por Sobre Todo Cuida tu Corazón*), comments:

> "Today our leaders look more like managers than pastors. Churches and the worship services resemble more and more the open markets, whose vendors, are brawling to sell their products. Pastors begin to abandon their posts, they have become celebrities, they turn into leaders with strong and dominating charismatic personalities, more like ecclesiastic executives than pastors of the flock of Jesus Christ...In this search for success and status they no longer have any time to build true and close friendships, there is no time for them to walk with their friends in the way of discipleship."[4]

On the other hand, some pastors have made of the pastorate their routine or "modus vivendi" (way of making a living), since they have focused their ministry on fulfilling functions, repeating programs, and basically carrying out a maintenance ministry without training others, without multiplying. Often these pastors are waiting for retirement time to come around, so then the district must take charge of the local church and see who is going to be the next pastor and take the church out of the mess it was left in.

The pastor disciple-discipler can provide the balance that is needed, since for him/her making disciples will become the heart of the mission and the essence of the pastoral ministry. This focus will make possible the reproduction and muliplication of him/herself in new pastors and lay leaders.

III. Discipleship in the New Testament included discipleship of pastors

Jesus discipled twelve laymen that became the apostles, the first pastors, of the church. Paul assigned and discipled lay pastors that he raised up in each place where he began the work among gentiles (Acts 14:20-23; 18:23).

> Jesus discipled twelve laymen that would become...the first pastors of the church.

IV. Priorities of the disciple making pastor

First, you need to reject the generic pastor model.[5]

Generic Pastor

- Considers himself the servant of the people. Instead of making disciples the pastor produces dependant, parasitic believers.
- Lets the church set the agenda, under the guise of being sensitive to their needs. He has no plan. This pastor has fallen under the dictatorship of the disobedient. The church has become a crazy place where immature, unskilled believers set the agenda for a highly motivated pastor.
- Accepts the church's role expectation concerning his time and activities. Too often this type of pastor does not have a specific understanding of himself and his role. Does a lot of things, but does not contribute to the most important thing: making disciples.
- Ministry strategy is circumstantial: it reacts to church conditions. He responds to the environment rather than creating it. He is worried about many details but is unable to filter and focus. He has lost sight of the big picture: the purpose of ministry.

Disciple Making Pastor

- Serves Christ, not the interests of the people, but seeks their best interest. The servant of Christ is dedicated to helping people do what they don't want to do so they can become what they have always wanted to be.
- Presents to the church his biblical agenda of making disciples, which he has embraced and will be the focus of his leadership in the church.
- Dedicates him/herself to sharing his vision for discipleship, and he focuses on equipping others, forming trainers.
- Maintains focus and rejects whatever does not contribute to fulfilling the mission of the church of making disciples and disciplers.

> **Group Exercise**
>
> How can pastors of local churches participate in continuous discipleship among themselves and with lay leaders? What difference would this make in the pastors' lives and in their pastoral ministry in the church?

Second, the pastor must see him/herself, not as a generalist, but as a specialist, as a pastor-teacher (disciplers) (Ephesians 4:11). "The reformation of professional pastoral work begins with the pastor's viewing himself as a specialist. His top priority as teacher/equipper is to get the work of ministry done through others. Doing it right means multiplication of ministry through every member.[6]

Third, the pastor maker of disciples will take the following steps :[7]

1. Preparation will be top priority. The maximum priority is the training of others. Provides the conditions, disciplines him/herself for this task and establishes an accountability system beginning with his own ministry.

2. Seeks proper identification of God's people. The disciple making pastor tells the people of God who they are and what his purpose is: to prepare them for the work of ministry.

3. Becomes pastor-teacher, not pastor-teller. Does not only communicate through preaching what we as a church should do (make disciples), but also teaches how to do it. Telling people what to do without providing the means to do it is cruel and disappointing. Over 90 percent of pastors must face the reality that preaching is not enough.

    The disciple making pastor follows the six steps that Jesus modeled in his teaching: "tell them what", "tell them why", "show them how", "do it with them", "let them do it", "deploy them (send them to do the same)."[8]

"the pastor must see him/herself, not as a generalist, but as a specialist, as a pastor-teacher (discipler)."

BILL HULL

4. Develops goal oriented leadership. The true test of goal orientation ability is not the original charting of the vision, but the management of the process over an extended period of time. The ability to keep the details of process on course over long chunks of time is goal-oriented leadership.

5. Creates a growing environment. To a great degree the attitude of the pastor will determine the attitude of the church. Three marks of the right environment:

    a. A strong sense of progress, taking risks and permitting people to make mistakes as they go forward.

    b. A commitment to "speak the truth in love" (Ephesians 4:15) and to persevere in their spiritual growth.

    c. A disposition to cooperate one with another, work together as one body.

Fourth, the disciple making pastor understands the big picture of discipleship as he/she makes the Kingdom the model, the cross as the means, the commission as the method and His second coming as the motive.[9]

Fifth, the disciple making pastor is committed to...[10]

1. Placing disciple making at the heart of the church.
2. A clear identification and communication of his/her role as pastor, of the people of God and of the discipleship process.
3. The priesthood of all believers.
4. Multiplication.

V. The pastor-builder of a community of disciples

The local pastor, in collaboration with his/her leaders and brothers and sisters, has the opportunity and the challenge of forming the church as a community of disciples so that when they come together as a congregation they are discipled together. The discipleship experience that the community of faith offers through the united activities such as communion, worship and service are powerful and help create an atmosphere for discipleship to take place at other times.

The pastor needs to intentionally and persistently work with the congregation, the local church board and the ministry leaders to develop a discipling congregation. "To become a discipling community, the church does not only have to experience the Lordship of the 'Kyrios', but must also live His presence...The church participates in the discipling task as it enjoys and cultivates the presence of the Lord." [11]

For the disciple making pastor to shape this kind of community he/she needs to take into consideration two things:

- **First**: Not to succumb to the constant temptation of guiding the ministry of the church to merely making converts instead of making disciples. "The church seduced by the currents of this world has lost the central focus of the pedagogical process of making disciples and to a large degree has embarked in the enterprise of merely making proselytes."[12]
- **Second**: Have as your vision and practice to guide the congregation so it can become a conscientious and growing community... [13]
    - that disciples through the Spirit
    - of trainers
    - that is united and renews itself
    - of ministers
    - of love

The distinctive mark of discipleship is the human relationships that are characterized by 'agape' love. In the measure that a disciple lives out his relationship with the Master, he also lives out that love in community. This love sustains in the midst of the search of the new identity as a disciple of Jesus, as it continues to grow and mature.

Conclusion

It should be unacceptable as pastor to carry out a local ministry without a discipleship ministry modeled and carried out with others.

Vocation in the New Testament is expressed in pastoral terms and with discipleship characteristics, since they are both intimately united with the person of Jesus. That is: "Vocation is to know Jesus, reproduce his actions, and imitate his works. This is precisely the mission that the elders or pastors should carry out in the Church." [14]

Let us recover the pastoral vocation as disciples-disciplers!

Integration Activity

1. What concrete steps can be taken so that each pastor can live out the biblical model of being a disciple making pastor?
2. How can the pastor begin to shape a discipling community of faith?
3. In what ways can the pastor's colleagues and other leaders support him/her to become a pastor-discipler?

Vocation is to know Jesus, reproduce his actions, and imitate his works.

Focusing...

Read the following memo* and answer the questions that follow

TO: Jesus, Son of Joseph
     Woodcrafter Carpenter Shop
     Nazareth

FROM: Jordan Management Consultants
      Jerusalem

Dear Sir:

Thank you for submitting the resumes of the twelve men you picked for management positions in your new organization. All of them have now taken our battery of tests; we have not only run the results through but also arranged personal interviews for each of them with our psychologist and vocational aptitude consultant.

It is the staff opinion that most of your nominees are lacking in background, education and vocational aptitude for the type of Enterprise you are undertaking. They do not have the team concept. We would recommend that you continue your search for persons of experience in managerial ability and proven capability.

Simon Peter is emotionally unstable and given to fits of temper. Andrew has absolutely no qualities of leadership. The two brothers, James and John, the sons of Zebedee, place personal interest above company loyalty. Thomas demonstrates a questioning attitude that would tend to undermine morale.

We feel that it is our duty to tell you that Matthew has been blacklisted by the Greater Jerusalem Better Business Bureau. James, the son of Alphaeus, and Thaddaeus definitely have radical leanings, and they both registered a high score on the manic-depressive scale.

One of the candidates, however, shows great potential. He is a man of ability and resourcefulness, meets people well, has a keen business mind and has contacts in high places. He is highly motivated, ambitious and responsible. We recommend Judas Iscariot as your controller and right-hand man. All of the other profiles are self-explanatory.

We wish you every success in your new venture.

Sincerely yours,

Jordan Management Consultants

In the light of this memo...

1. What do you think of this analysis of the twelve disciples Jesus chose? What factors contributed to the transformation in their lives through their discipleship process?
2. How do you see yourself as a pastor or leader of a ministry?
3. What would be your evaluation of your ministry as a pastor or lay leader?
4. What steps do you need to take to reorient your ministry to more effectively disciple and train others who are part of the church?
5. What persons would you choose to help you guide the church in the life-long discipleship process?
6. What would you do as a layperson or pastor so you can become a maker of disciples and leaders for the church?

* Greg Ogden, Transforming Discipleship, Dowers Grove, IL: InterVarsity Press, 2003: 77.

Lesson 6

Discipleship for everybody

General Objective

Assist the trainers in catching the vision for a holistic discipleship ministry, where making disciples is the heart of the church.

Lesson Summary
- Discipleship for the whole person.
- Discipleship for all ages.
- Discipleship for the different stages and crises of life.
- Discipleship through all the ministries of the church.

Key verse to memorize

"Pointing to his disciples, he said, here are my mother and my brothers.... Jesus called his disciples to him and said, 'I have compassion for these people; they have already been with me three days and have nothing to eat. I do not want to send them away hungry, or they may collapse on the way'" (Matthew 12:49; 15:32, NIV).

Introduction

Discipleship in the local church is not for a select group of people. Since making disciples is the heart of the mission of the church, each member of the Body of Christ should contribute. For this reason, the church should focus its ministry on a holistic discipleship of all people and families.

I. The church needs to focus its Discipleship on the whole person

The biblical vision of human beings is that they are total persons with body, mind, emotions, moral and social qualities integrated by the Spirit (1 Thessalonians 5:23). The development of Jesus' discipleship was far reaching, including a wide range of activities: instruction, modeling, spiritual disciplines, human relationships, family, roles and responsibilities, multiplication and participation in small groups, etc. It is necessary to grow every day in some of these aspects of our lives in the likeness of our Master and making his mission our own.

II. The church should have and make disciples among all age groups: children, young people and adults, men as well as women

Jesus' call to be his disciples is extended to children as much as to young people and adults of all ages.

Group Exercise

Discipleship begins when someone surrenders their life to Jesus. Can a child take this step? What elements would be different in the discipleship of a child in contrast with a young person or an adult?

Jesus' call to be his disciples is extended to children as well as to young people and adults of all ages. That is why we need to train disciplers for children, young people, adults, women, men and even married couples.

Who are the ideal persons to disciple persons among these different ages?

47

> The crises and changes in the different stages of life can become a time to deepen our relationship with God...

First, we should consider the leaders among these age groups as disciplers, but we should also train other disciplers from within the groups. Even with children, if it is possible, it would be good that another child that is more mature can accompany a leader that will disciple children so he/she can be trained as a future discipler.

Besides, it is recommended that the people of the same sex disciple each other. This will allow for more intimate and open relationships. That is, men disciple men, and young girls or women disciple other females. It would also be better to combine one on one discipleship with discipleship in a small group.

It would be beneficial if occasionally we disciple in the church through inter-generational groups, and whole families: children, young people, adults and the elderly. Those who do not have family members in the church could be adopted by a family. We should remember that the Christian families need to strengthen themselves through times of spiritual growth together.

III. Discipleship in the different stages and crises of life

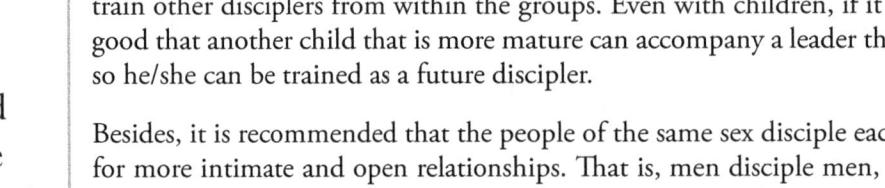

Group Exercise

Share briefly about the different crises you had in past years. What changes have these crises brought to your life? From whom have you received support? Was the church ready to help you in these crises? Have the crises prepared you to help others later on?

As we have observed, discipleship is much more than just classes for those who have just received Christ as their savior. We need to make the whole church aware of the importance of discipleship in all the stages of our lives. The different stages, as well as the crises in life, bring changes, which in turn could result in uncertainty, confusion, fear and a sense of being unable to face these situations.

Accompanying our brothers and sisters in the church through a discipleship process that is based on the Word of God, along with emotional support and concrete actions, will turn the crisis into a means of growth and maturity. In this way, the crises and changes in the different stages of life can become a time to deepen our relationship with God, as we get to know him more intimately and we are strengthen in our faith.

Let us prepare to disciple in the transitions of life, and how they affect the different members of the family, such as in times of:

- a pregnancy and the coming of a new baby
- the beginning of school for a child
- the teenage years
- choosing studies for a career or profession
- getting married
- workplace tensions
- when children leave the home (empty nest)
- the middle age crisis
- retirement age crisis

Let us prepare to disciple in the unexpected circumstances of life:

- illness: terminal and chronic disease
- death
- loss of job
- accidents
- separation, divorce
- unwanted pregnancy
- natural disasters

Feeling the support of the church in the midst of these crises reinforces the bonds of brotherhood and the commitment to serve others. When the church provides its people with an intentional discipleship in midst of the different circumstances they have to face, it gives them security and a sense of belonging to the Body of Christ.

IV. The church should integrate all its ministries so they can intentionally contribute in the formation of disciples and disciplers

> **Group Exercise**
> What is a ministry? Why are there diverse ministries in the church? What ministries are active in your local church? In what ministries do your participate?

A ministry is an opportunity of service through the church, utilizing spiritual gifts given by God through the Spirit.

The goal of each ministry in the church should be to use their unique strategies and resources to make holistic disciples. Therefore, the mission of making disciples becomes the heart of the church, integrating all the ministries of the church and giving them vitality and direction.

A wide range of ministries are necessary in the church since we need to develop holistic disciples that are:*

- **Compassionate**: contributing to the physical and material needs of people (Nazarene Compassion Ministries, NCM)
- **Global**: with a vision and participation in the work around the world (Nazarene Missions International, NMI).
- **Students**: weekly learning from the Word of God —of all ages— so they can live the gospel (Sunday School and Discipleship Ministries, SDMI).
- **Youth**: that they can be formed by Christ from their youth and impact their generation reaching young people and discipling them (Nazarene Youth International, NYI).
- **Disciplers**: disciples with the commitment of investing time, energy, and their teaching abilities to instruct and accompany others (Discipleship Ministry).
- **Reaching new disciples**: living and sharing the gospel (Evangelism).
- **Leaders**: used by God through their lives and ministries to influence others for Christ (Leadership Ministry).
- **Worshippers**: exalt God through their lives and are an integral part of the church in its corporate worship (Worship Ministry).
- **Pastor-disciples**: fulfilling their pastoral call as they focus on developing the church as a community of disciples-disciplers and developing new pastors (Pastoral Ministry).
- **Educators**: through their participation in theological education or any other educational ministry in the local church they train other disciples so they can carry out their ministry efficiently. Teach Christian Education in the local church (Theological Education).

> The goal of each ministry in the church should be to use their unique strategies and resources to make holistic disciples.

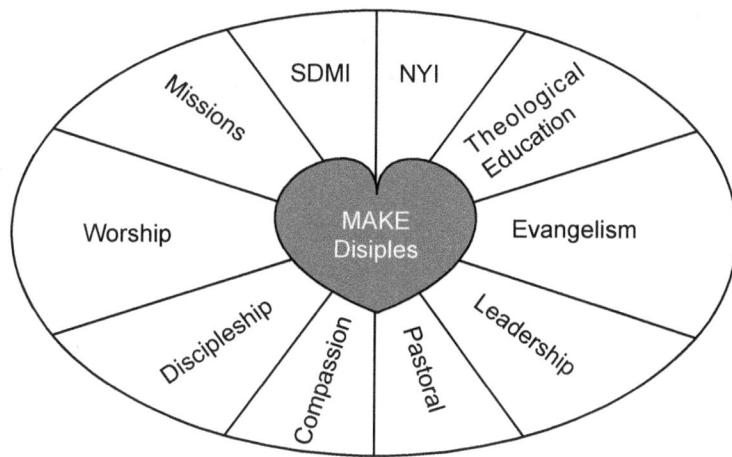

* In parenthesis are ministries that are carried out in the Church of the Nazarene.

Conclusion

Discipleship is for everybody. As it has been described, it will help us grow and together stretch ourselves as disciples-disciplers in the church. It will bring unity of purpose and spiritual vitality to the church, and effectiveness and community in our mission to the world. In this way, the Spirit will become an integrating agent.

Integration Activity

1. How can we get each ministry to be focused on contributing to make disciples and disciplers? Share three ideas.
2. Give your testimonies related to how some churches are able to focus their different ministries on making disciples.

Focusing...

Discipleship for all: Placing discipleship in the heart of the local church

One of the commitments of the disciple making pastor, and even of the local leaders, should be to put discipleship at the heart of the church. There are three indispensable actions that the pastor must carry out so this can take place:

1. Proclaim from the pulpit, the priority that discipleship is for the church.
2. Write it down and make it church dogma. Writing down your discipleship will constantly remind and motivate the church.
3. Model disciple making at the leadership level. Most people in the church need to see something in action before they can understand and embrace it.*

Pastors of churches with highly effective discipleship ministries can recommend to churches that are interested in upgrading their level of discipleship that they...**

- Recognize that disciple-making is a process, not a program. It is about building people...more important than anything else is to develop a church-wide culture that values becoming a disciple.
- The process will not occur without leadership from the senior pastor. The lay leaders may be able move the process forward, but the weight of the senior pastor's commitment to personal spiritual growth is required to initiate the process.
- The church's ministry focus must be streamlined to prioritize and support discipleship. That includes establishing genuine spiritual growth as a core element of the church's mission and eliminating programs and ministries that divert people´s attention and the church's resources.
- The process is not likely to succeed unless there is a simple but intelligent plan for growth.
- The process will not generate true disciples unless it has a designated supervisor to facilitate progress.
- In creating a process that works, adapt lessons learned by other effective disciple-making churches to your own unique ministry context.
- Be prepared for burnout and complacency to set in after two or three years of involvement in an intensive process. This tendency to depart from the process can be diffused by building a ministry environment in which almost everyone is involved in discipleship.
- Carefully balance the competing interests of flexibility and structure.

Discuss the following application questions:

1. How feasible are these principles to refocus the pastoral and lay ministry to making disciples?
2. What practical steps can you take to center the ministry of your church in your context on making disciples?
3. Which of the above suggestions represent the greatest challenge for your ministry as a pastor or as a lay leader?
4. On which of the above steps have you been working on to place making disciples as the heart of the church? What has been the reaction of the congregation and other leaders?

---

* Bill Hull, The Disciple-Making Pastor, Grand Rapids, MI: Fleming H. Revell, 2004: 117-121.
** George Barna, Growing True Disciples, Ventura, CA: Issachar Resources, 2004: 101-103.

Lesson 7
Discipleship in the family

> **General Objective**
>
> Show the trainers the importance of discipleship in and with the family as one of the key elements of the discipleship ministry in the church.
>
> **Lesson Summary**
> - Discipleship through the family in the Old Testament.
> - Discipleship in the family according to Jesus and the New Testament church.
> - Challenges for discipleship in the family.
> - Important questions about the family for the new disciple.
> - Suggestions to initiate family discipleship in the home and in the church.
> - Discipleship in the family from the Wesleyan heritage.
>
> **Key verse to memorize**
>
> "These commandments that I give you today are to be upon your hearts. Impress them on your children. Talk about them when you sit at home and when you walk along the road, when you lie down and when you get up. Tie them as symbols on your hands and bind them on your foreheads. Write them on the doorframes of your houses and on your gates." (Deuteronomy 6:6-9, NIV)

"In the Old Testament, discipleship as faith formation was the direct and prime responsibility of both parents."

Introduction

Since biblical discipleship is centered on relationships, not only knowledge, we should disciple through groups, not just individually. The basic small group that forms society and the church is the family, the home.

The family, like other small groups, is a greenhouse, a place where relationships are cultivated: first our vital relationship with Christ and then our relationships with those around us as part of our testimony and life. As we are discipled together with our families we establish deep relationships of intimacy and friendship.

Group Exercise

How have you grown spiritually in your family since you gave your life to Christ? Do you know a family that does discipleship from the home? If so, Do you notice any difference in them?

In the church we need to return to a discipleship that is more biblical so we can form communities and families of disciples. Also, church in its totality needs to be discipled as the family of God (Galatians 6:10, Ephesians 2:19). This is the model we observe in the Old and New Testament.

I. Discipleship through the family in the Old Testament

Through the people of the Old Testament, discipleship as faith formation was the direct and prime responsibility of both parents as the core of the family (Deuteronomy 4:9-10 y 6:7-9). This home discipleship was complemented by the work of the priests and other teachers of the law.

Already in Genesis 12:1-3 God had called Abram along with his family saying, "'Leave your country, your people and your father's household and go to the land I will show you. I will make you into a great nation and I will bless you; I will make your name great, and you will be a blessing. I will bless those who bless you, and whoever curses you I will curse; and all peoples on earth will be blessed through you. (NIV)'" To bless implies, among other things, to teach and guide the families to faithfully follow God.

In his farewell speech, Joshua challenges the families of Israel to be faithful to their God, and ends by calling his people to make a decision: "But if serving the LORD seems undesirable to you, then choose for yourselves this day whom you will serve,...But as for me and my household, we will serve the LORD." (Joshua 24:15). This is a commitment that Joshua makes publically, to continue influencing his family so that they will serve God. This is the central aspect of discipleship in the family, and to which Joshua invited all the families of the people of God.

II. Discipleship in the family according to Jesus and the New Testament church

It is interesting that when Jesus talks about discipleship and the family, he focuses more on the urgent need to follow him beyond the family. (Matthew 4:22; 8:21-22; 10:35-37; 12:8-30; Luke 14:20, 26; 18:29). Yet, Jesus chose the Twelve and formed an alternative family to carry out his specific mission, without his disciples and himself completely leaving their own families.

Also, Jesus supports the obligation of children to their elderly parents (Mark 7:6-13) and he valued their marriage relationships (Mark 10:2-12). He even proposes the family relationships as a model for his disciples (Mark 3:31-35; 10:28-20). The gospels also record the fact that Jesus sent his disciples to proclaim the good news of the Kingdom in the homes (Mark 6:10), and the news that he and his disciples were received by some families (Mark 11:11; 14,3). [1]

> "While you are going, MAKE DISCIPLES, of ALL THE FAMILIES of the earth."

The Great Commission mandate of making disciples of all nations has as its background, the call of Abraham to be a blessing to "all the families of the earth". The word "nations" in Matthew 28:19 means "ethnic groups", not nations in the contemporary sense. Ethnic groups are people groups or clans of families with their own distinctive characteristics and cultures. So the Great Commission can be understood as: "while you are going, MAKE DISCIPLES, of ALL THE FAMILIES of the earth."

The early church also started discipling and doing ministry through families in their homes (Acts 5:42). That is why the persecution of the church was focused on families (Acts 8:3). We also notice in Acts, various family conversions and baptisms (Acts 16:30-34; 16:14-15; 18:8). This emphasis on family discipleship continues with examples like Timothy (2 Timothy 1:5), and when Paul requires that the bishops, deacons and elders manage their own families well (1 Timothy 3:4-5, 12; Titus 1:6).

III. Challenges for discipleship in the family

Group Exercise

Review the following challenges of discipleship in the family. With which ones do you identify the most and which of these have been major obstacles for discipleship in the families of your church?

1. Many parents are unaware of their responsibility in the spiritual growth of their children since they did not receive this example from the home they grew up in.
2. Most parents were not personally discipled when they began their walk with Christ, so they lack the basic knowledge and experience.
3. Some parents have not been exposed in the church to family models where family members grow in their faith through collective and individual discipleship in the home.
4. Carelessness, laziness and lack of perseverance.

5. Not organizing well family time or letting each member go their own way, especially teens and young people.
6. The family devotional time becomes routine and lacks creativity and flexibility, becoming just a "mini church service at home".
7. The family members are absorbed by work and don't make time to meet.
8. The lack of commitment by the married couple to involve their children in family discipleship.
9. The use of, and the loss of time, viewing programs that do not edify children as well as adults.
10. Bad relationships between husband and wife, parents and children, brothers and sisters, that creates a counterproductive atmosphere for discipleship.
11. The lack of an example from the parents in their personal discipleship and as a couple.
12. The family does not have goals for their spiritual lives and for service to others.
13. Involvement in good activities but that takes up a lot of time; such as sports, celebrations and even family reunions. Time should be used wisely in these types of activities.
14. Goals and plans for the family that are not bad as such, but, if we are not careful, can displace spiritual growth in the family. For example, focusing on: making more money, having more things, and other goals. Even the good ambitions that parents have for their sons and daughters: like studying in the university, become professionals, etc. can become excuses for not developing discipleship in the family.
15. The church and the pastor have not prioritized the family as a key element of discipleship in the church.

"...as parents, we need to be and live as disciples of Christ so we can make disciples of our sons and daughters."

IV. Important questions about the family for the new disciples (converts) that we need to consider so we can focus better our discipleship process through the church:

1. From what type of family do they come: dysfunctional or healthy? How are their relationships with the family members close to them? His/her spouse, children and extended family.
2. How can the family relationships improve as a result of their decision to follow Christ?
3. Is there someone in the family with whom they need reconciliation?
4. If they are living together, are they legally married?
5. How can the new disciples testify to their family members about their new life in Christ? How can we train them for this?
6. How can we reach the whole family of the new disciples? How can we as a church minister to the whole family?

V. Suggestions to initiate family discipleship in the home and in the church

We can begin with some of the following practical and simple things: [2]

- First of all, parents need to be and live as disciples of Christ so they can make disciples of their sons and daughters. Love, compassion, understanding and patience are necessary along with the firmness of our convictions.
- Read the Bible and pray together as a family, applying the Word of God to the different ages and interests of your children. It is not necessary to be too "religious" in this time together but create an atmosphere of trust and transparency.
- Eat together as much as possible and talk around the table about the interests of each member—especially those of the children—making comments from a biblical perspective.

- Spend time together during the weekends and holidays, taking advantage of this time to bring biblical teaching related to what we experience together.
- Carry out work projects around the house.
- Motivate and supervise the personal devotional time of each member of the family. The personal and family devotional times prepare us for collective worship in the church.
- Practice the spiritual disciplines together as a family: prayer, fasting, meditation, and others.
- Develop an intimate relationship with each child, spending individual time with each one and talking about their things and issues so the parents can help them apply the Word of God to their personal lives. Mom and dad should oversee the spiritual growth of their marriage and of their sons and daughters.
- Do sports, play table games and other fun things as a family. If you watch TV or a film together, discuss what you have seen in the light of the Word of God so you can discern what is good and bad and provide guidelines for the family members.
- Celebrate the Lord's Day as a different day from the rest of the days of the week, so that this time can be vital for discipleship in the home.
- Challenge the church, as a "family of families", about the urgent need of developing a discipleship ministry for and from the family.

VI. Discipleship in the family from the Wesleyan heritage

Our Wesleyan heritage, whose founders were the Wesley family, spearheaded by John and Charles Wesley, provides guidelines and examples for discipleship in the family. There are two key elements of the Wesleyan movement that we will consider:

a. The home life of the Wesleys in eighteenth century England.
b. The organization in small groups for the nurture and development of the fruit of the Wesleyan movement.

Susanna Wesley, the mother of John and Charles Wesley, was the prime source of instruction and inspiration. She made up her mind that she would change the world and reach others, beginning with "take[ing] a more than ordinary care of the souls of her children." [3] She was committed and dedicated herself to her family's spiritual formation of faith—family discipleship—since she was aware that some day she would have to give an account to God as a steward of her children.

She set apart two hours regularly for her daily devotions alone with God. Susanna made this decision when she already had nine children. She had a total of 19 children in 23 years. Susanna Wesley strongly emphasized that the main task in bringing up her children was to help them conquer their will early in life and thus have an obedient temper. This would produce fruit in their intellectual development as well as in their inclination towards piety and the spiritual life.

After John Wesley began his open air preaching ministry he "began to organize the new converts in societies that met in homes during the week to worship, pray, study the Bible and support each other." [4]

They would also meet in smaller groups called "classes" to deepen their faith and give offerings for the poor. It was this organization into small groups that helped with the discipleship of the new members and in their preparation they would later become the leaders of the societies and even lay pastors and evangelists. [5]

They sang the doctrine in their family meetings, since Charles Wesley had written hymns for this purpose. As resources for the families, John Wesley included in his writings: A collection of forms of prayer for every day in the week, A collection of prayers for families, Prayers for Children and A scheme of self-examination. [6]

Susanna Wesley made up her mind that she would change the world and reach others beginning with "take[ing] a more than ordinary care of the souls of her children..."

Nobody else but parents can disciple their children while they are living in their homes.

Conclusion

How can we bring together discipleship and the family?

We have to be willing to make some sacrifices so that discipleship in the family can become a reality, yet to "talk about family discipleship without sacrifice makes no sense in modern life." [7]

The church and Christian parents should be convinced that if we do not carry out this type of home-based discipleship nobody else will, and our children will lack the divine teachings that will guide their lives towards God. Nobody else but the parents can disciple their children while they are living in their homes. Christian schools, the programs of the church, Christian children's clubs, etc., can help, but they cannot be a ubstitute for the home and the time of family discipleship. [8]

Discipleship in the family has two important implications for the ministry of the church:

1. That the church intentionally operates as the family of God, that is, as the "family of families". That the church focus on the holistic growth of the families, and that together with the parents it contributes to discipling all the members and families. It is the church that should disciple through its groups and when together as a congregation.
2. That the discipleship ministry in the church be channeled through the family nucleus, and thus develop a pastoral ministry to the families with the purpose of making disciples of them.

There is no limit to what God can do through only one family. How much more if we are many families being formed, with the help of God and the full support of the church so we can fulfill our mission of being and making disciples of all the families of the earth.

We have the example of the Wesley family: "God prepared a family and especially a mother (Susana) and one of her sons (John), who in the hands of God and filled with the Holy Spirit, changed the course of the history of his country and continues to influence the history of the world." [9]

Integration Activity

1. How can you begin family discipleship in your church? What changes are necessary to implement family discipleship in your congregation?
2. How would you work with the Christian homes of the church to involve everyone in a discipleship that is focused on the family? What difference would this type of discipleship make in the church?

Focusing...

Family Discipleship in the Wesleyan Tradition

Let us look once again at discipleship in the family through the Wesleyan tradition. Susanna Wesley carried out a number of activities aiming at the faith development of her family. These practices became positive habits that with time fostered spiritual values in her children. They include the following, just to name a few:*

- When turned a year old, (and some before,) they were taught to fear the rod, and to cry softly.
- At six p.m., as soon as family prayers were over, they had their supper; at seven in the evening, the maid washed them; and beginning at the youngest, she undressed and got them all to bed by eight p.m.
- Each day, except for Sundays, Susanna dedicated six hours to the moral instruction of her three sons and seven daughters.
- The children were taught, the Lord's Prayer as soon as they could speak, which they were made to say at rising and bed-time each day.
- In the mornings they read a Psalm and a chapter of the Old Testament. Then they went to their private prayers before having breakfast or meeting as a family.
- Susana decided to set apart one hour per week to be alone with each one of her children to have a conversation with them about their spiritual life.
- Early on, before they could well speak or walk, they were taught to distinguish the Sabbath from other days.
- During Sunday afternoons, Susanna directed her family in doing works of piety and devotion, additional instruction of the Word. At the end of the day they celebrated a family service in the house.

Application questions:

1. What do you think about these practices, although they are from eighteenth century England?

   _____

   _____

2. Which of Susanna Wesley's practices with her children catches your attention the most?

   _____

   _____

3. What biblical and family discipleship principles can you see behind these practices?

   _____

   _____

4. What more contemporary practices, according to your life setting, can you implement for effective discipleship in today's family?

   _____

   _____

---

* Works of Wesley, Volume I, A letter from Susanna Wesley to her son John dated July 24, 1732: 387-393.

Lesson 8

Discipleship Strategy for the local church

General Objective

That trainers can develop a strategy to help their local church implement or develop even more the local discipleship ministry.

Lesson Summary

- The process of the development of a strategy: Diagnosis, Mission and Vision, Goal and Objectives, Action Plan, Implementation and Supervision, Periodical Evaluation and Strategy Renewal.
- Three stages to implement the discipleship ministry.
- Example of a discipleship strategy from the Church of the Nazarene in the Mesoamerica Region. *

Key verse to memorize

"They preached the good news in that city and won a large number of disciples. Then they returned to Lystra, Iconium and Antioch, strengthening the disciples and encouraging them to remain true to the faith. We must go through many hardships to enter the kingdom of God," they said. Paul and Barnabas appointed elders for them in each church and, with prayer and fasting, committed them to the Lord, in whom they had put their trust." (Acts 14:21-23, NIV).

> " A strategy is an action plan that helps us implement principles...with the purpose of fulfilling our mission and vision"

Group Exercise

What is a strategy? How can a strategy help us develop a discipleship ministry in the local church?

Introduction

A strategy is an action plan that helps us implement principles one step at a time with the purpose of fulfilling our mission and vision. As trainers for the discipleship ministry in the local church, we need to determine how we are going to implement what we have learned. For this we will need to develop a strategy.

I. The process of the elaboration of a strategy

The following elements should be worked on, in the prescribed order, to develop a discipleship strategy for the local church:

a. Diagnostic - *Where do we find ourselves as a church regarding discipleship?*

What are we already doing in discipleship? What is the vision of the pastor and lay leaders for discipleship in the local churches? What are the obstacles for a dynamic and growing discipleship ministry? How can we expand our focus in the discipleship ministry to incorporate the vast biblical foundations?

b. Mission and vision - *The main purpose of discipleship and where does God want to lead us?*

What is the mission —why we exist— and the vision —the better future we foresee— for the discipleship ministry in light of the biblical foundations, the needs of the church in our setting? Begin

---

* The Mesoamerica Region of the Church of the Nazarene includes the Caribbean, Mexico, Central America, and Panama.

to involve the church in prayer focused on discerning a mission and a clear vision from God for the local discipleship ministry. Then, develop, together with other leaders in the church, a mission and vision statement for the discipleship ministry.

c. Goals and objectives - *Steps towards fulfilling the discipleship mission and vision*

What are the general objectives that we wish to accomplish through the discipleship ministry in the local church? What are the specific goals we have determined to reach those objectives in six months, a year, and yearly for the next five years?

d. Action plan - *Concrete process by stages to make and multiply disciples*

What type of planning will we need to carry out this process? Which persons will we count on or need to involve in the process? How can we generate and channel financial resources for this project? Which concrete steps will be taken to begin and then follow to reach the goals and objectives? We suggest you work on the discipleship process in the following three stages: basic, intermediate and advanced discipleship (see the following point in this lesson).

e. Implementation and supervision - *Initial steps and building the discipleship process*

What will the first and the following steps be in the implementation of the strategy? How will you train and motivate leaders of the local church? Who will accompany and guide the church in the process of building your discipleship ministry?

f. Periodical evaluation - *Constant revisions and adjustments of the discipleship process*

You will need to evaluate the progress of the strategy in different points in time in the process taking into consideration which are your goals. When, how and with who will you carry out these evaluations?

> The discipleship strategy is the link between the biblical principles of discipleship and actual discipleship in the life of the church.

Group Exercise

Taking into account these steps explained above, How would you initiate or develop a strategy for your present discipleship ministry in the church?

g. Strategy renewal - *Evaluation of effectiveness of strategy over time, possible change of strategy*

As a result of your evaluations you may see the need of adding some other elements to the strategy. After using the strategy effectively for some time, when it is no longer feasible or productive, you might even consider replacing the present strategy for another one.

The discipleship strategy is the link between the biblical principles of discipleship and discipleship as the life of the church.

Discipleship Principles
Intentional
Interpersonal
Intergenerational
Interminable
Integral
Intertwined
Integrator

Strategy
Diagnosis
Mission and Vision
Goal and Objectives
Action Plans
Implementation & Supervision
Periodic Evaluation
Strategy Renewal

Life of the Church
Being and Building
a community of disciples

II. Three Phases or stages to implement the discipleship ministry

In order to develop and implement an intentional, lifelong discipleship strategy as part of your action plan, it is recommended that you consider the three major discipleship phases: basic, intermediate and advanced discipleship.

In general terms, you could organize the basic discipleship phase to run from the conversion of new believers, going through the preparation for baptism, and ending with church membership. The intermediate discipleship phase could guide the new member of the church to continue growing, and among other things, begin to discover their spiritual gifts and involve them in a ministry in the church. The advanced discipleship phase could concentrate on the development of leaders for the ministries and advancement of the church. This includes training disciplers for children, youth, adults, couples and families in the church. This last phase is open so that the church can continue adding whatever is necessary for the on-going (life-long) discipleship journey.

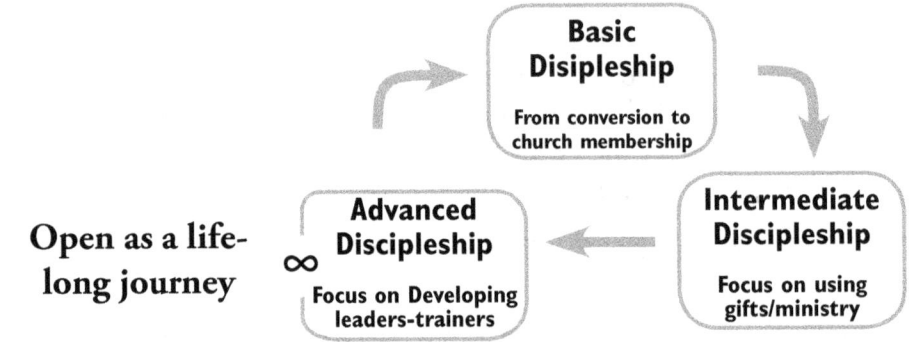

Putting this system in writing will provide a sequential discipleship strategy that will build on previous phases and guide the disciples towards maturity and multiplication. In the same way that the normal human being grows from one phase to another until he/she becomes a parent (adult) that reproduces, we could guide disciples in the church from their birth, to maturity and reproductivity, and until their last day of life.

We need to organize these three major discipleship phases including at least four key elements in each one: (1) biblical teachings, (2) activities or events, (3) materials you will use and (4) integrate the age level ministries (for children, youth and adults) in the process (see the charts in the Focusing sheet at the end of this lesson). Within this system you should include in the process discipleship for children, young people, and adults that can also be focused towards discipleship among women, men, couples and families. We need to avoid falling into the trap of developing a discipleship system only for adults and carrying out isolated efforts in discipleship disconnected one from another, that is, without a system.

But this is only a blueprint for the discipleship ministry. After this you will need to start building, little by little, each of the discipleship phases until you have developed the whole system in an average of 4-5 years.

There are two key elements that you need to insert at some point in the process: (1) the vision for multiplication, and (2) the selection and training of disciplers for children, young people, and adults: women, men, couples and even families. Disciplers can be started in their training in the intermediate discipleship phase as they discover they have gifts for discipling others (discipleship will be their ministry) and continue developing in the advanced phase of discipleship and beyond.

We need to continuously work on both extremes of the discipleship process and consider our discipleship plan even before people give their lives to Christ, (normally understood as evangelism) and also have a discipleship system that is open to the future (continuously upgrading). Following these principles, the discipleship process can start with bible studies with contacts that do not yet know Christ, expecting that along the way God will touch them and they will surrender their lives to Christ, and the discipleship process continues with them, as new disciples. On the other end, in the advanced discipleship phase, new themes, activities and materials should be added, according to the needs and situations that occur in the local church and in the setting.

This discipleship strategy is more focused on the new converts so that they can be involved in a life-long process from the beginning of their faith in Christ. But before or during the development of this discipleship system, you initiate some changes in the brothers and sisters who are already part of the church who will prepare the way for this continual process (see Lesson 10, Specific steps to initiate and develop a discipleship ministry in the local church, page 73):

III. Example of a discipleship strategy from the Church of the Nazarene in the Mesoamerica Region

The following is an example of a discipleship strategy that has been used by the Mesoamerica Region in the Church of the Nazarene, which involves the churches in the Caribbean, Mexico and Central America:

Three basic dimensions:

TO BE: like Christ, attaining to the whole measure of the fullness of Christ, in His image, being transformed from glory to glory.

TO KNOW: about God, his ways, the history of his people, our doctrine, our church and organization, our tradition.

TO DO: his will through ministry, exercising our spiritual gifts.

How can we accomplish this? Through life-long discipleship:

- Discipling the new converts
- Training believers to carry out their spiritual gifts
- Training those called to ministry
- Perfecting the saints
- Training the trainers

Five levels of discipleship, ABCDE Discipleship Process (Ephesians 4:16)

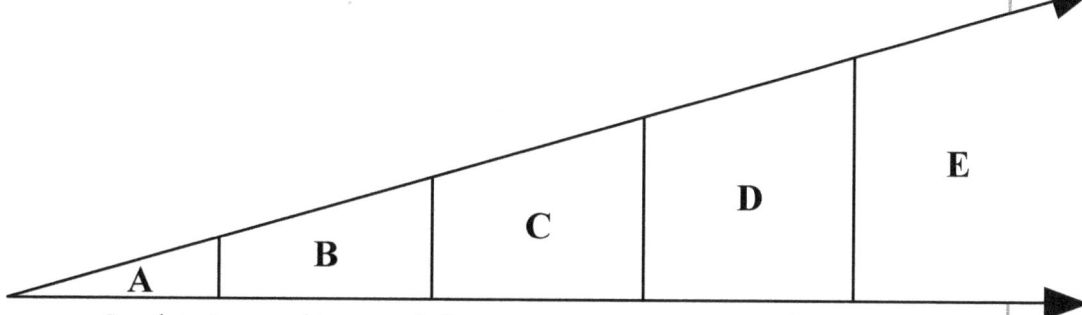

- Level A: Approaching non-believers, pre-conversion, evangelism.
- Level B: Baptism to entire sanctification, from conversion to church membership.
- Level C: Consolidation, life-long learning through the local ministries of the church.
- Level D: Development of ministry, training lay ministers.
- Level E: Education of leadership, School of leadership (in the local church or for professional ministry).

Training Courses: Tools for this process, training courses (TC in sequence from 1 to 3):

TC1: Discovering my place in the local church: a broad view of the diverse ministries in the church through introductory workshops.

TC2: Discovering the committed: basic training for leaders of the different ministries.

TC3: Consolidating the ministers: a one-year training program to prepare local ministers in each ministry (School of Leadership): Worship, Administration and Leadership, Compassion, Discipleship, Evangelism, Young People, Sunday School, Missions/NMI (Nazarene Missions International), and Pastoral ministry.

Conclusion

The purpose of the development of a strategy is that each local church can have a continuous and effective discipleship ministry to carry out the mission of making disciples through your ministry and through the new churches that are planted.

But above all, develop a simple discipleship system. "Being simple requires seeing the whole picture…To have a simple church, leaders must ensure that everything their church does fits together to produce life change. They must design a simple process that pulls everything together, a simple process that moves people toward spiritual maturity." [1]

Integration Activity

Use the Focusing sheet at the end of the lesson to determine how useful these steps are for developing your local discipleship strategy.

Focusing...

Design Your Local Discipleship System

Design the discipleship system of your local church, for children, young people and adults, filling in the following phases of discipleship and the four elements shown in each one.

DISCIPLESHIP BEFORE CONVERSION			
Biblical Teachings	**Activities**	**Materials**	**Ministries**

BASIC DISCIPLESHIP (NEW DISCIPLES)			
Biblical Teachings	**Activities**	**Materials**	**Ministries**

INTERMEDIATE DISCIPLESHIP			
Biblical Teachings	**Activities**	**Materials**	**Ministries**

ADVANCED DISCIPLESHIP			
Biblical Teachings	**Activities**	**Materials**	**Ministries**

Maybe you began developing your discipleship system for adults in the local church, but you can use this same format to develop your discipleship system for children and young people.

Lesson 9

Using discipleship materials

> **General objective**
>
> Provide the trainers with guidelines for selecting and organizing materials that will be a part of the local strategy to carry out an effective discipleship ministry.
>
> **Lesson summary**
>
> - Materials as tools for discipleship.
> - Basic criteria for choosing discipleship materials.
> - Organize the materials as part of the discipleship strategy.
> - List of books and resources on discipleship for training and working with groups.
>
> **Key verse to memorize**
>
> "Then the LORD replied: 'Write down the revelation (vision) and make it plain on tablets so that a herald may run with it. (Habakkuk 2:2)

Introduction

Materials, books and other resources are useful in developing an intentional, life-long discipleship ministry. Yet, we should not make the mistake of putting the focus of the process of discipleship solely on acquiring published materials. Materials by themselves do not assure the development of good disciples. The excessive dependency on materials and literature for discipleship is common among many church leaders.

It is necessary to select the best materials for discipleship, but we should not fool ourselves: no material is better than the persons that use them. We should center the discipleship ministry on personal relationships and, in this way, seek a dynamic and healthy relationship between disciples and disciplers. Let us remember that the manual par excellence for discipleship has always been the Bible. Whether we have abundant additional materials or we lack them because we do not have enough money or for other reasons, the Bible needs to be our main resource.

We also need to find ways to utilize other printed, visual, and audio materials for the many persons that learn orally because it is their need or because it is their preference. At the present, there are approximately "four billion oral communicators of the world: people who can't, don't, or won't take in new information or communicate by literate means. Oral communicators are found in every cultural group in the world and they constitute approximately two-thirds of the world population!" [1] This makes oral discipleship one of the most urgent needs of our times.

I. Materials as tools for discipleship

Materials are necessary tools for the discipleship ministry and we need to use them. We should be familiar with them and know what each one is used for. It is important that we make sure that the content of the materials coincides with our theology, our belief system.

It is necessary to select the best materials for discipleship.

The materials —besides the fact that they help us in our immediate task of the discipleship ministry in our local churches— should inspire us as we consider the local needs and motivate us to use our creativity to develop our own materials. The materials that we prepare locally, after going through the rigor of our practice, can be shared with others.

Although materials are valuable tools, we should not lose sight of the importance of the quality of life of the disciplers who will use them. What materials did Jesus, the primitive church and Paul use to disciple? Are they not the outstanding biblical examples for our discipleship today? They did not even have a complete Bible. But they did permit God to use their lives filled with the Holy Spirit, their obedience and availability for God, and the resources they had within their reach.

Finally, it is necessary that the disciplers, through practice, ongoing training, and evaluation of their task, acquire greater skills in their use of the discipleship materials. In so doing, discipling others individually and/or in groups is carried out with greater effectiveness and others will learn to disciple in the process.

> **Group Exercise**
> 1. How can a mechanic repair a motor without tools?
> 2. What would happen if a doctor performed an operation without the right tools?

II. Basic Criteria for choosing discipleship materials

CONTENT	The doctrinal and theological focus should agree with what you believe as a church regarding God, human beings, salvation and the Christian life.	☐
USE OF THE BIBLE	The material should have abundant biblical verses and passages, although it should also include other important elements of spiritual formation.	☐
USEFULNESS	We should ask ourselves, will this material meet the spiritual and life needs of the disciples in our church? Can it be easily understood?	☐
RELEVANCE	The material, although it needs to include principles, should be focused on helping disciples follow Christ in the midst of the reality of daily life. So that, discipleship becomes a way in which the disciples can incorporate what is learned in their web of relationships.	☐
PARTICIPATION	What is the degree of participation that is required of the disciple(s) through the use of this material?	☐
	What type of preparation will the discipler need to have to guide the discipleship process with this material?	☐
TIME	What amount of time is expected to be invested in this material during the week and in the meeting with the discipler or group?	☐
FOCUS	Is the material designed to be used one-on-one, in groups or both?	☐
DIFFERENT TYPES OF MATERIALS	You will need materials for the different stages of discipleship, the different age groups, and for different discipleship groups.	☐
USE FOR DISCIPLERS	Can you utilize this material to train new or more advanced disciplers?	☐
PRESENTATION	The physical presentation of the material should be attractive so it could invite us to read its content.	☐
PRICE	The local church as well as the disciples needs to invest in discipleship materials. The price should be reasonable so people can buy it.	☐

Discipleship materials abound; they are found in bookstores, through different ministries and on the Internet. It becomes important to have basic criteria for choosing the best materials for the discipleship ministry in your local church.

The table above provides some guidelines so you can choose the discipleship materials for your church:

Any material that is developed outside of the local church should be adapted to the specific needs of the local church. If we utilize materials that coincide with our theology we will have to make fewer adjustments.

> **Group Exercise**
>
> What materials do you use as tools to carry out the discipleship ministry in your local church? Which of the criteria mentioned above has become your priority as you select discipleship materials?

III. Organize the materials as part of the discipleship strategy

The materials that will be used should be organized in a sequence within the different stages of discipleship, along with the other suggested elements that should be part of your discipleship system or strategy (See Focusing, p. 8, at the end of lesson # 8 on discipleship strategy). We include the following design that will help you place the materials in the order that they will be used:

	MATERIALS FOR DISCIPLESHIP			
	Discipleship before conversion	Basic Discipleship	Intermediate Discipleship	Advanced Discipleship
Children				
Teens/Young People				
Adults (Women and Men)				

To acquire discipleship materials we need to teach and challenge our church to invest money to have these tools, since this should be a priority for the church. A financial budget will need to be prepared, and different and creative means to raise the necessary funds will need to be developed. You may receive offerings and periodical donations, carry out activities to raise funds, ask for financial contributions from parents of children and young people, establish a partnership system for the disciples, and other means.

You need to emphasize that the discipleship materials will not be an expenditure of the church, but an investment in the formation of the present and future disciples and disciplers who will carry out the mission of the church. We should call people to contribute to this cause with joy and generosity.

IV. Books and resources on discipleship for training and working with groups

An important part of the development of a discipleship strategy for the local church is the recruitment and training of disciplers and leaders for the discipleship ministry.

For this important task one also needs to use adequate materials. The development of the training of these trainers should be carried out in two levels with their respective materials:

1. The constant task of formation and multiplication of disciplers: qualified persons who disciple and guide the discipleship process of children, young people, adults, women and men in the church,

2. leaders who train disciplers and other trainers. At the same time, they will develop the discipleship ministry through the development of a strategy, according to the needs of the church. These leaders will put in motion a vision for the multiplication of disciples and disciplers.

The following is a list of books from which you can choose for training in discipleship, and some can be used in small groups:

Anderson, Leith. Jesus: An Intimate Portrait of the Man, His Land, and His People. Minneapolis: Bethany House, 2005.

Barclay, William. Discovering Jesus. Louisville: Westminster John Knox Press, 2000.

Barna, George. Growing True Disciples. California: Issachar Resources, 2000.

Bennett, Ron. Intentional Disciplemaking. Colorado Springs: Navpress, 2001. (www.navpress.org)

Boyett, Joseph & Jimmie. The Guru Guide: The Best Ideas of the Top Management Thinkers. New York: John Wiley & Sons, Inc., 1998.

Camp, Lee C. Mere Discipleship: Radical Christianity in a Rebellious World. Grand Rapids: Brazos Press, 2003.

Coleman, Robert E. The Great Commission Lifestyle. Grand Rapid: Fleming H. Revell, 1992.

_____. The Master Plan of Discipleship. Grand Rapid: Fleming H. Revell, 1998.

_____. The Master Plan of Evangelism. Grand Rapid: Fleming H. Revell, 2002.

Dorsey, Jim. Best Practices in Discipleship: Renewing our Missional Heritage. Kansas City: Evangelism Ministries, 2006.

Drury, Keith. Spiritual Disciplines for Ordinary People. Indianapolis: Wesleyan Publishing House, 2004.

Foster, Richard. Celebration of Discipline: The Path to Spiritual Growth. New York: Harper Collins Publishers, 1998.

_____ & James Bryan Smith. Devotional Classics: Revised Edition: Selected Readings for Individuals and Groups. New York: Renovaré, 1993.

Goodwin, Debbie Salter. Raising Kids to Extraordinary Faith: Helping Parents & Teachers Disciple the Next Generation. Kansas, City: Beacon Hill Press, 2008.

Henderson, D. Michael. Making Disciples One Conversation at a Time. Kansas City: Beacon Hill Press, 2007.

Hull, Bill. Choose the Life. Grand Rapids: Baker Books, 2004.

_____. The Complete Book of Discipleship: On Being and Making Followers of Christ. Colorado Springs: NavPress, 2006.

_____. The Disciple-Making Church. Grand Rapids: Fleming H. Revell, 1990.

_____. The Disciple-Making Pastor. Grand Rapids: Fleming H. Revell, 1988.

_____. Jesus Christ, Disciple Maker. Grand Rapids: Baker Books, 2004 (www.bakerbooks.com).

ION/LCWE. Making Disciples of Oral Learners. Bangalore, India: Sudhindra, 2005.

Koessler, John. True Discipleship: The Art of Following Jesus. Chicago: Moody Publishers, 2003.

Matthaei, Sondra Higgins. Making Disciples: Faith Formation in the Wesleyan Tradition. Nashville: Abingdon Press, 2000.

McDonald, Glenn. The Disciple Making Church: From Dry Bones to Spiritual Vitality. Grand Haven, MI: Faith Walk Publishing, 2004.

McDowell, Josh & Kevin Johnson. Josh McDowell's One Year Book of Family Devotions. Wheaton, IL: Tyndale House Publishers, 2003.

McLaren, Brian D. More Ready Than You Realize. Grand Rapids: Zondervan, 2002.

Miller, Darrow L. Discipling Nations: The Power of Truth to Transform Cultures. Scottsdale, Arizona: Food for the Hungry, 1998.

MacArthur, John. Twelve Ordinary Men. Nashville: W Publishing Group, 2002.

Macchia, Stephen A. Becoming a Healthy Disciple. Grand Rapid: Baker Books, 2004.

MacDonald, William. True Discipleship. Port Colborne, ON, Canada: Gospel Folio Press, 2003.

McBirnie, William Steward. The Search for the Twelve Apostles. Wheaton, IL: Tyndale House Publishers, 1973.

Moore, Beth. The Beloved Disciple. Nashville: Broadman & Holman Publishers, 2003.

_____. Jesus, the One and Only. Nashville: Broadman & Holman Publishers, 2002.

Moore, Waylon B. New Testament Follow-up. Grand Rapids, MI: William B. Eerdmans Company, 1975.

Ogden, Greg. Discipleship Essentials. Downers Grove, IL: InterVarsity Press, 1998. (www.christianbook.com).

O'Grady, John F. Disciples and Leaders: The Origins of Christian Ministry in the New Testament. Mahwah, New Jersey: Paulist Press, 1991.

Ortiz, Juan Carlos. Disciple: A Handbook for New Believers. Lake Mary, FL: Charisma House, 1995.

Perkins, Hal. Walk With Me: A Biblical Journey in Making Disciples. Kansas City: Beacon Hill Press, 2008.

Petersen, Jim. Lifestyle Discipleship: The Challenge of Following Jesus in Today's World. Colorado Springs: Navpress, 1993.

Peterson, Eugene H. A Long Obedience in the Same Direction: Discipleship in an Instant Society. Downers Grove, IL: InterVarsity Press, 2000.

Reyenga, Henry Jr. The Spontaneous Spread of Home-Discipleship Christianity. Monee, IL: Home Discipleship Press, 2006. (www.homediscipleship.org)

Sanders, J. Oswald. Real Discipleship. Grand Rapids: Zondervan Publishing House, 1974.

Schultz, Joani. Fun Excuses to Talk about God Devotional Guide. Loveland, CO: Group Publishing, Inc., 1998.

Stowell, Joseph M. Following Christ. Grand Rapids, MI: Zondervan Ublishing House, 1996.

Watson, David Lowes. Forming Christian Disciples. Nashville: Discipleship Resources, 1991.

Watson, Kevin M. A Blueprint for Discipleship: Wesley's General Rules as a Guide for Christian Living. Nashville: Upper Room Press, 2009.

Wilkins, Michael J. Following the Master: A Biblical Theology of Discipleship. Grand Rapids: Zondervan Publishing House, 1992.

Willard, Dallas. The Great Omission: Reclaiming Jesus' Essential Teachings on Discipleship. New York: Harper Collins Publishers, 2006.

Zodhiates, Spiros. Discipleship. Chattanooga, TN: AMG Publishers, 1999.

Advanced Discipleship (Training in Leadership)

Barna, George. The Power of Vision: Discover and Apply God's Vision for Your Life & Ministry. Ventura, CA: Regal Books, 2003.

Blackaby, Henry & Richard. Spiritual Leadership: Moving People on to God's Agenda. Nashville: Broadman & Holman Publishers, 2001.

Blanchard, Ken & Phil Hodges. Lead Like Jesus: Lessons from the Greatest Leadership Role Model of All Time. Nashville: Thomas Nelson, Inc., 2005.

Covey, Stephen R. Seven Habits of Highly Effective People. New York: Free Press, 2004.

Engstrom, Ted W. The Making of a Christian Leader. Grand Rapids: Zondervan Publishing House, 1977.

Haggai, John. The Influential Leader: 12 Steps to Igniting Visionary Decision Making. Eugene, OR: Harvest House Publishers, 2009.

Maxwell, John. The 21 Irrefutable Laws of Leadership: Follow Them and People Will Follow You. Nashville: Thomas Nelson Inc., 1998.

_____. The 360 Degree Leader: Developing Your Influence from Anywhere in the Organization. Nashville: Thomas Nelson Inc., 1998.

_____. Becoming a Person of Influence: How to Positively Impact the Lives of Others. Nashville: Thomas Nelson Inc., 1997.

_____. Developing the Leaders Around You: How to Help Others Reach Their Full Potential. Nashville: Thomas Nelson Inc., 1995.

_____. Developing the Leader Within You. Nashville: Thomas Nelson Inc., 1993.

Sanders, Oswald J. Spiritual Leadership: Principles of Excellence for Every Believer. Chicago: Moody Bible Institute, 1994.

Swindoll, Charles R. Improving Your Serve. Nashville: W Publishing Group, 1981.

Youssef, Michael. The Leadership Style of Jesus: How to Develop the Leadership Qualities of the Good Shepherd. Wheaton: Victor Books, 1986.

Classical Discipleship Books

Bonhoeffer, Dietrich. The Cost of Discipleship. New York: Macmillan Publishing Co. Inc., 1961.

Bruce, A. B. The Training of the Twelve (1894). Grand Rapids: Kregel Publications, 1988 (Two Volumes).

Kempis, Thomas. The Imitation of Christ: How Jesus Wants Us to Live. New York: Harper Collins Publishers, 2000.

Lewis, C. S. Mere Christianity. New York: Harper Collins Publishers, 1980.

Stott, John R. W. Basic Christianity. Grand Rapids: William B. Eerdmans Publishing Company, 1971.

Conclusion

Discipleship materials and literature can be very useful in our mission of multiplying disciples and disciplers. It is important to know and select which resources will be more effective in each phase of continuous and holistic discipleship. Because of the vast variety of available materials, it is crucial that one knows how to select and use the necessary materials to develop your local discipleship strategy.

Integration Activity

1. Which of the aspects related to the selection of materials represent major challenges that your local church faces?
2. What steps would you take with the church to invest in materials for discipleship?
3. How would you raise the funds needed to purchase the necessary discipleship materials?

Focusing...

Utilize the following criteria to evaluate your disciplers and their continual development.

Characteristics of the discipler/leader for the discipleship ministry		
Spiritual life	Daily and systematically is nurtured through the Word of God and develops a life of fervent prayer. Participates in spiritual retreats and the means of grace, such as, personal and collective fasting, the Lord's Supper and other spiritual disciplines.	☐
Family Relationships	Enjoys a healthy marriage relationship (if married), and cultivates good relationships with children and close family members, such as parents, brothers and sisters, and with other extended family members.	☐
Participation in the life of the church	As a member of the church attends the services and activities. Is faithful in giving his/her tithes and offerings, contributes to the financial support of the church. Loves the brothers and sisters and leaders of the church, and participates in fellowship with them. Agrees with the doctrines of the church he/she is affiliated to.	☐
Personal Qualities	Is mature, loving and respects the persons and their different opinions. Is balanced, sober, and humble, accepts help from others for his/her personal growth. Is usually on time and fulfills his/her responsibilities.	☐
Discipleship Vision	Has an ample and holistic vision of biblical discipleship. Is convinced of the central and indispensable nature of the mandate of making life-long disciples for the church and to fulfill its mission in the world. Is open to change and is willing to pursue it for the well-being of the church.	☐
Multiplication in discipleship	Is committed to the principle of the multiplication of disciples, disciplers and leaders for the discipleship ministry. Is propelled by a vision for multiplication and constantly shares this vision with those he/she carries out ministry and with the church.	☐
Skills for ministry	Is patient and perseveres, works the discipleship process at the rhythm of each disciple. Is willing to be corrected in love. Is a good teacher and guide; has ample knowledge of the Word and of its interpretation and application for daily life. Focuses his/her instruction on the training of persons so they can grow personally and utilizes activities and other dynamic means as a discipler.	☐
Group leadership	Cultivates his/her basic abilities to conduct a discipleship group and uses his/her influence to develop persons within an atmosphere of camaraderie and mutual support. Is a part of the team of the other disciplers.	☐
Organizational Abilities	Is disciplined, inspires others to imitate this life-style. Has the ability for organizing and focusing his/her time, materials, teachings and follows the adopted discipleship system.	☐
Constant growth	Is constantly trained in his knowledge, skills and commitments by the leaders of the discipleship ministry and/or the pastor. Continues to enhance his/her life-long learning.	☐

Have you thought of some people from your church that meet the majority of these characteristics so you can invite them to be trained as disciplers? Write down their names:

_____

_____

_____

What materials will you use to train them initially and during the process?

_____

_____

Some books that can help you train disciplers:

Collins, Steven. Christian Discipleship: A Step-by-Step Guide to Fulfilling the Great Commission. Tulsa, OK: Hensley Publishing, 1989.

Bill Hull. The Complete Book of Discipleship: On Being and Making Followers of Christ. Colorado Springs: NavPress, 2006.

Leroy Eims. The Lost Art of Disciple Making. Grand Rapids: Zondervan Publishing House, 1978.

Gregory Ogden. Transforming Discipleship: Making Disciples a Few at a Time. Downers Grove, IL: InterVarsity Press, 2003.

Gary W. Kuhne. Dynamics of Discipleship Training. Grand Rapids: Zondervan Publishing House, 1978.

Ron Bennett & John Purvis. The Adventure of Discipling Others: Training in the Art of Disciplemaking. Colorado Springs: NavPress, 2003.

Lesson 10

How to develop a discipleship ministry

General Objective

Share with the trainers some practical guidelines on how to initiate or develop discipleship ministry in different situations in the local churches.

Lesson Summary

- The gap between what Scriptures says and what we see in the church.
- General guidelines to begin and carry out a discipleship ministry in the local church.
- Specific steps to initiate and develop a discipleship ministry in the local church.
- Things you should avoid.
- Suggestions to develop a support ministry for discipleship for the local church.

Key verse to memorize

"And he directed the people to sit down on the grass. Taking the five loaves and the two fish and looking up to heaven, he gave thanks and broke the loaves. Then he gave them to the disciples, and the disciples gave them to the people" (Matthew 14:19).

The product that Jesus requires from the church is a person called a disciple.

Introduction

In general, the people of the church are being discipled by the culture that surrounds them. Specifically, television and the mass means of communication are discipling the people of our countries. "The people sitting in the pews are products of television more than the Word of God. Their world views are not scripturally based; rather they are disciples of their culture" [1]

Greg Ogden describes the state of discipleship in the church of the United States with the word superficiality [2] (growth in numbers without depth). Bill Hull, mentions that "the crisis at the heart of the church is a crisis of product. What kind of persons does the church produce? The Christ-commanded product is a person called a disciple." [3]

Then the problem is not the world but the church, specifically the quality of its discipleship. The cardiovascular system of the church is the principles that produce the right product: disciples-disciplers.

Discipleship and the true nature of the gospel should propel our evangelism. In this way, how we reach the new believers and help them grow as followers of Jesus in the church will clear the way for our ongoing discipleship.

If we are going to carry out a dynamic discipleship ministry based on the biblical model, we need to analyze where our local churches really are and in what direction God wants them to go. Therefore, "if we are to devise a successful strategy of disciple making in our churches, we must first assess the gap between where we are and where we are called to go." [4] The church can no longer stay as it is, it needs to change.

Discipleship and the true nature of the Gospel should propel our evangelism.

I. The gap between what we find in Scriptures and what we see in the church [5]

The Scriptural Vision	The Church Today
A church with...	A church with...
1. Proactive Ministers.	1. Passive recipients.
2. A spiritually disciplined life-style.	2. Spiritually undisciplined, where few invest in their spiritual growth.
3. Holistic discipleship that affects all of life.	3. Private discipleship, focused only in the sphere of faith and it merely becomes a personal and private matter.
4. Countercultural force.	4. Blending in life-style and values similar or identical to non-Christians.
5. An attitude that the church is essential, chosen by God as his instrument to extend his kingdom	5. Attitude that being the church is optional and even unnecessary.
6. Biblically informed people.	6. Biblical illiterate, the Bible is an unknown book.
7. People sharing their faith.	7. Shrinking from personal witness, avoid sharing their testimony.

II. General guidelines to initiate and develop a discipleship ministry in the local church

> **Group Exercise**
>
> What is the reality of your local church and other churches around you regarding discipleship ministry? What things do you believe need to change?

1. Constant prayer, both individually and with the leaders of the church and the congregation, in order to carry out an effective discipleship ministry.
2. Establish the discipleship ministry on a strong biblical foundation.
3. Change our own mentality, the mentality of leaders and brothers and sisters regarding the discipleship ministry of the church; return to the holistic biblical, vision for discipleship.
4. It is crucial that the conviction of the pastor be that discipleship is central to the mission of the church and that he/she declare it as top priority from the pulpit [6] and teach this to all the groups of the church.
5. That discipleship is established as the criteria to measure the success of the church. [7]
6. Model the disciple-making philosophy at the leadership level of the church. The pastor and the leaders should be effective disciple makers themselves. [8]
7. Gear the task of the local board so it could become a small group for spiritual growth to guide and facilitate making disciples (the mission) as the unifying center of all the ministries in the church.
8. Refocus the role of the pastor so that his/her main function becomes making and training others as disciplers of disciplers. The lay leaders need to let the pastor guide the church in this way while he/she continues to be accountable to them.
9. Channel funds to the discipleship ministry.
10. Plan for long term discipleship ministry. The implementation of this ministry in the local church usually requires a minimum of five years. [9] A long term commitment to this ministry is required of the pastor and the church. A discipleship ministry should be initiated with the intention of leaving it well rooted in time.
11. Take the Great Commission seriously as pastor. "The major issue in taking the Great Commission seriously is the intentional guidance of the church leadership towards mul-

"That discipleship is established as the criteria to measure the success of the church."

BILL HULL

tiplication. A process must take people from conversion to trained disciple maker. This should occupy a great deal of the leadership's time and creative energy. [10]

12. Prepare for opposition. As pastors and leaders that desire to begin an effective discipleship ministry in your local church, you will soon feel the opposition. Like any significant change in the church, many will not understand from the beginning since changes tend to create certain instability that make people uneasy. That is why there is resistance from the outset.

"Disciple making takes more faith than any other task of the church. Since it is the top priority for God, it is the top priority for Satan to stop it. No work of God's servant draws more resistance than disciple making...The disciple-making pastor will be resisted; a spiritual war will be waged." [11]

III. Specific guidelines to initiate and develop a discipleship ministry in the local church

Group Exercise

What specific steps would you take to implement and develop a discipleship ministry in your local church? If someone has lived this process, he/she can share how it has gone.

There are no two churches alike, and each local congregation is living a different moment in its life, but all churches have been called to make disciples. The following are some guidelines to develop a discipleship ministry in the church. As pastor or lay leader, choose and emphasize from the following practices the one or two that are most useful for you.

With the present church: Prepare the church so it can walk through the path of discipleship immediately inserting some strategic changes as the basis for the discipleship system that will be developed later. In order to guide the church in this direction you could ...

- Initiate a time of intense prayer with the church board and with the congregation seeking direction from God so you can center the ministry of the church in its mission of making disciples.

- As pastor, choose a mentor or select a support group of lay leaders for your spiritual growth and be accountable to them in the areas of your personal life. Besides the benefit of this help as a pastor, you will also be modeling discipleship yourself.

- Involve the whole congregation in the basic discipleship training that you will use for new converts. While you are in this process you can recruit disciplers for all ages.

- Preach a series of sermons from biblical passages about being and making disciples. You can go through a book in the Bible or share discipleship themes from different texts.

- Lead Bible studies with the church or in small groups regarding discipleship.

- Include in the Sunday School classes or lessons on discipleship during a trimester or for six months. You can use this Handbook for Discipleship Training for this means.

- Organize the local church board in small groups focused on their spiritual growth and make the spiritual development of these key leaders a priority. In so doing, you are training the leaders of the church board so they can contribute to the spiritual growth of the other leaders with which they are carrying out their ministries.

- Carry out spiritual retreats for the different sectors of the church and for the leaders, emphasizing on their lives and ministry as disciples and disciplers.

"Disciple making takes more faith than any other task of the church. Since it is top priority for God, it is top priority for Satan to stop it."

BILL HULL

Towards the future in the discipleship ministry:

- Start removing the obstacles for discipleship related to the mentality of the leaders and congregation, with their renewed spiritual condition and healthy interpersonal relationships among the members of the church.
- Make formation of the persons in the church a high priority, more than simply running programs and doing projects. Cultivate healthy and growing relationships.
- Initiate the discipleship strategy or plan for your church, evaluating where you are in the local discipleship ministry. Does it exist? What is its focus? Is it only oriented towards instruction? Is it partial, only for new converts or to receive new church members? Are your discipleship efforts organized in a system by stages that are known by the congregation? Is there spiritual life and constant transformations taking place among your people? How can the local discipleship ministry improve and be more dynamic?
- Design a blueprint. With the leaders of the church elaborate and put in writing a discipleship system that you want to build for children, young people and adults. Develop the three phases of discipleship with its elements. You can use the suggested steps for putting together a strategy in lesson 8, pages 58-62. Depending on the reality of each church, the process of putting this in writing usually takes from 3-6 months or a little longer.
- Implement a stage or phase of discipleship at a time. Begin providing the basic discipleship stage and training disciplers. Elaborate not only instruction, but other dimensions of holistic discipleship, including the social aspect (compassion). Then continue implementing the other phases of discipleship, with their respective adjustments in the process, until you have progressively completed the whole system.
- Foster a multiplication mentality and atmosphere.
- Consider the use of small groups for discipleship and evangelism.
- Focus and integrate all the ministries of the church so they can contribute to making holistic disciples. Strengthen and expand the ministries permitting new ministries to be born according to the needs and gifts of the persons.
- Build up the evangelism ministry to reach new disciples. Involve everyone in diverse forms of evangelism.
- In periodical meetings with leaders give priority to evaluating the effectiveness and progress of the discipleship ministry.
- Create alternative structures that do not substitute or go against the "official" structure of the church but facilitate expanding and empowering the discipleship ministry.
- Constantly train, motivate and make adjustments in the process.

IV. Things you should avoid

1. Do not begin big, trying to put together the whole discipleship system quickly or too soon. Take the necessary time to prepare laypersons, selecting key, mature persons that are willing to continue growing through the discipleship experience. You can begin with a small group of leaders that you will invite, but with an ample vision for intentional discipleship that is multi-level and multi-generational.
2. Do not initiate small groups without specific purposes and without a covenant that makes the members accountable one to the other and committed to invest in their spiritual growth and involvement in service to others.
3. Do not turn discipleship into another program of the church.
4. Do not present the idea of discipleship before the church board for its approval. Remember that to "make disciples" is the mandate of the Master for the church; we cannot decide not to do it.
5. Do not fall into the temptation of quick multiplication. You need to begin the process, but you need to give it enough time so you can develop disciples that are formed

holistically. Do not give way to the immediate or what is easier. "The key to a disciple-making ministry is the willingness of the people to delay gratification. It takes five years to establish a discipleship ministry that flows and that bears fruit within the church." [12]

6. Do not fall prey to pragmatism, only worried with whatever works, or with what immediately yields a large amount of people, nor with what people like without considering if what is done in discipleship has biblical foundations.
7. Do not center the ministry in "feeling", nor water down the demand of the Word of God. Do not talk only of the benefits of the gospel. Share the costs as well.
8. Do not assume that the programs, services and activities of the church will automatically produce disciples. To make disciples requires that we intentionally refocus everything the church does so it can contribute to making disciples, and make use of other more personalized means, like small groups so that persons can be formed into authentic disciples of Jesus.

V. Suggestions to develop a support ministry for discipleship for the local churches

Following are some ideas for a district or judicatory to organize the discipleship ministry and its leaders can support this ministry in the existing and new local churches:

1. The district/judicatory should focus its ministry on the development and channeling of resources to the local churches.
2. All the ministries of the district/judicatory should focus on contributing with their resources, tools and programs towards making disciples.
3. Evangelism and discipleship ministries need to work together.
4. Appoint, according to spiritual gifts, a district/judicatory discipleship committee; its coordinator could also be a part of the district/judicatory evangelism committee.
5. Provide training and motivation for the discipleship ministry of the local churches.
6. Facilitate and elaborate discipleship materials.
7. Utilize the discipleship ministry as the foundation of the development of leaders.

Conclusion

The discipleship principles should be incorporated in the life of the local church through an effective discipleship ministry with its strategy and leaders who are dedicated to this important task. Let us make the necessary changes so that making disciples becomes the center of the church model we have, and in this fashion, we can produce what Christ ordered: disciples in His likeness in all the nations. Jesus —through his Spirit—has promised to be with us and support us directly, as long as we are actively and consistently involved in this precious task.

"Simple church leaders are designers. They design opportunities for spiritual growth…The simple church leaders we surveyed were expert designers…They have skillfully designed an environment where life change is likely to occur. They have designed a simple process that moves people through stages of spiritual growth…Church leaders struggle with implementing a process. In fact, church leaders admit that this is their biggest ministry struggle." [13]

Integration Activity

1. How should we pray to implement and develop the discipleship ministry in the local church?
2. What role does unity in the church play so we can develop a project of intentional discipleship?
3. What would be the best way for the district or judicatory leadership to facilitate the discipleship ministry in the local churches?

Let us work hand in hand with our Master and Lord of the Church, so we can grow and develop as His disciples, and systematically help others to grow along with us! And when the Lord returns, he can find us being faithful to His mandate of making Christlike disciples!

Focusing...

How can a church in the following situations be guided to develop an intentional, dynamic and life-long discipleship ministry?

- Church that has never had a discipleship ministry.

- Church with discipleship only for new converts.

- Church with discipleship oriented solely to make new members.

- Church in crisis.

- Church which has not been organized around different ministries.

- Church centered in services and special events.

- Church that focuses discipleship only as the transmission of knowledge.

- Church that does not work with small groups.

- Church with discipleship only to prepare leaders for small groups.

- Church with a good amount of people but without a discipleship ministry.

- A new church plant.

End Notes

Lesson 1:

1. Bill Hull. *The Disciple-Making Pastor.* Grand Rapids: Fleming H. Revell, 2004: 54.
2. Michael J. Wilkins. *Following the Master: Discipleship in the Steps of Jesus.* Grand Rapids: Zondervan Publishing House, 1992: 25-34 (http://www.apcod.org/apcod2003/articles/article_wilkins1.html).
3. Wilkins, 26-27. Note 6 at the bottom of the page. A variation on this view suggests that discipleship was appropriate to Jesus' day, while people could follow him around physically, but that today, since Jesus has ascended to heaven and believers can no longer follow him physically, it is inappropriate for us to speak of ourselves as disciples (Wilkins, footnote # 6, 26-27).
4. Juan Carlos Ortiz, *Disciple,* Carol Stream, IL: Creation House, 1975, 9.
5. Wilkins, 27-28 (Dwight Pentecost, Design of Discipleship. Grand Rapids: Zondervan, 1971:14)
6. Wilkins, 29 (Paul Minear, "The Disciples and the Crowds in the Gospel of Matthew," AThR Sup. Series, 3 March 1974:31).
7. Wilkins, 30 (McGarvran y Arn. *How to Grow a Church.* Glendale, CA: Gospel Light, 1973; C. Peter Wagner, *Stop the World I Want To Get On.* Glendale, CA: Regal, 1974:79)
8. Wilkins, 31 (Dietrich Bonheoffer, *The Cost of Discipleship,* trans. R. H. Fuller, 2d rev. ed. New York: Macmillan,. 1963:47, 60)
9. Wilkins, 34-39.
10. Wilkins, 39-42.

Lesson 2:

1. Wilkins, 51-69.
2. Hull, 50.
3. Roberto J. Suderman. *Discipulado Cristiano al Servicio del Reino* (Christian Discipleship at the Service of the Kingdom). Bogotá: Ediciones Semilla-Clara, s/f: 10, 44.
4. Suderman, 11.
5. Suderman, 12-13.
6. Coleman, Robert. *The Great Commission Lifestyle.* Grand Rapids: Fleming H. Revell, 1992. This book is divided in three principal components, so they are elaborated with greater detail in this book.
7. Hull, 15.
8. C. René Padilla. *Bases Bíblicas de la Misión: Perspectivas Latinoamericanas* (Biblical foundations of the Mission: Latin American Perspectives). Grand Rapids: Eerdmans Publishing Co., 1998, Chapter 1 by Sydney Rooy, "La Búsqueda Histórica de las Bases Bíblicas de la Misión (The Historic Search of the Biblical Foundations of the Mission)", 7.

9. Mariano Ávila y Manfred Grellert, *Conversión y Discipleship* (Conversion and Discipleship). San José: Visión Mundial Internacional, 1993: 89-91 and Chapter 4 by Jorge Maldonado, "La Iglesia Como Comunidad Discipuladora (The Church as a Discipling Community) ", 72-73.
10. Ávila y Grellert, Chapter 5 by Pedro Savage, "La Iglesia Como Comunidad Discipuladora del Reino (The Church as a Discipling Community of the Kingdom)", 92.
11. Ávila y Grellert, Chapter 5, 92.
12. Ávila y Grellert, Chapter 5, 93.
13. Ávila y Grellert, Chapter 5, 94. Five expressions of the radical nature of Jesus' discipleship call: (1) A rediscovery of the purposes of God and the rejection of the accumulated traditions of the "elders". (2) A critical labor begins of the society and culture in which one lives, being liberated little by little from the grip of those concepts and values that contradict the values of the Kingdom and the will of its Kyrios (Lord). (3) A process begins of living that new society. (4) The radical call is presented as a call to live in the present, in the world, in the light of the consummation of the Kingdom, the arrival of the King. (5) The radical call is a call to suffer (Mariano Ávila y Manfred Grellert, Conversión y Discipleship (Conversion and Discipleship). San José: Visión Mundial Internacional, 1993: 95-96).
14. Ávila y Grellert, Chapter 3 by Orlando E. Costas, "La Misión Como Discipulado (The Mission as discipleship)", 63.
15. Summary of Wilkins, 174-240.
16. Hull, 57.
17. Ávila y Grellert, Chapter 4, 79.
18. Greg Ogden. *Transforming Discipleship: Making Disciples a Few at a Time.* Downers Grove, IL: InterVarsity Press, 2003:100.
19. Ogden, 100.

Lesson 3:

1. Wesley Tracy, Morris Weigelt, Dee Freeborn, Janine Tartaglia, *The Upward Call: Spiritual Formation and the Holy Life*. Kansas City: Beacon Hill Press of Kansas City, 1994, 12.
2. Richard Foster. *Celebration of Discipline*. NY: Harper Collins Publishers, 1978:1.
3. Henry J. M. Nouwen. *Bread For the Journey.* Harper Collins Publishers, 1997: 60.
4. Suderman, 61-65.
5. Suderman, 65.
6. E. M. Bounds. *Power Through Prayer.* Radford, VA: Wilder Publications, 2009: 7-8.

Lesson 4:

1. Ogden, 136, quotes Gary Kunhe from "Follow-up—An Overview," in *Discipleship: The Best Writing from the Most Experienced Disciple Makers* (Grand Rapids, MI: Zondervan, 1981: 248).
2. Ávila y Grellert, Chapter 5, 87.
3. Robert Coleman. *The Master Plan of Discipleship.* Old Tappan, NJ: Fleming H. Revell Co., 1987: 39-40. Also see notes 16-19 and Phillip Schaff, History of the Christian Church, Vol. 1. Grand Rapids, MI: Wm. B. Eerdmans, 1950: 196-197.
4. Hull, 133.
5. Hull, 133.
6. Ogden, 69.
7. Ogden, 69.
8. Hull, 135-141. In these pages the author briefly explains each one of these points.
9. Ogden, 197.

10. Christian A. Schwarz. *Natural Church Development: A Guide to Eight Essential Qualities of Healthy Churches.* Carol Stream, IL: Church Smart Resources, 1998: 68.
11. Ávila y Grellert, Chapter 4 by Jorge Maldonado, 78.
12. Ron Bennett. *Intentional Disciplemaking.* Colorado Springs: Navpress, 2001: 72.
13. Bennett, 74. Author cites James Rutz from *The Open Church.* Auburn, MA: The SeedSower, 1992: 47.
14. Hull, 173.
15. Bennett, 75.
16. Bennett, 81. In the first part of this quote the author cites Paul Stanley & Robert Clinton in *Connecting* and the second part of the quote he cites Howard & William Hendricks in *As Iron Sharpens Iron.*
17. Ogden, 140-142. In these pages the author briefly explains each one of the following points.
18. Ogden, 149-152. Each one of these are described in these pages.
19. Ogden, 145.
20. Ogden, 146-149.
21. Ogden, 15.
22. Christian A. Schwarz y Christoph Schalk: *Implementation Guide to Natural Church Development.* Carol Stream, IL: Church Smart Resources, 1998: 97.
23. Bennett, 78-79.
24. Schwarz & Schalk, 98-102.
25. José H. Prado Flores. *Formación de Discípulos* (Formation of Disciples). México: Publicaciones Kerygma, 2005:187.

Lesson 5:

1. LeRoy Eims. *The Lost Art of Disciple Making.* Grand Rapids: Zondervan Publishing House, 1978: 11-12.
2. Eims, 12.
3. Eims, 17.
4. Ricardo Barbosa de Sousa. *Por Sobre Todo Cuida tu Corazón* (Above All Guard Your Heart). Buenos Aires: Ediciones Kairos, 2005:172, 173.
5. Hull, 80-83. By generic the author means, "general, nonspecific, or plain…general and plain in purpose and goal". The generic pastor is in many ways the exact opposite of the disciple-making pastor.
6. Hull, 88.
7. Hull, 92-103.
8. Hull, 190-202.
9. Hull, chapter 5: 104-116.
10. Hull, chapter 6: 117-145.
11. Ávila y Grellert, chapter 4, 106.
12. Ávila y Grellert, 81. Also see chapter 5, 104-105.
13. Ávila y Grellert, 107-112.
14. Carlos María Martín. *La vocación en la Biblia* [Vocation in the Bible]. Salamanca: Ediciones Sígueme, 2002: 125.

Lesson 7:

1. La renuncia a la Familia de Jesús y sus discipulos (Jesus' self-renunciation of his family and disciples), en www.jesus.teologia.upsa.es/subsecciones.asp?codsubseccion=99.
2. Some of these ideas come from Samuel Clark, in the article Discipulado en el Hogar (Discipleship in the Home) in http://www.losnavegantes.net/discipuladofamiliar.html.

3. Sondra Higgins Matthaei. *Making Disciples: Faith Formation in the Wesleyan Tradition.* Nashville: Abingdon Press, 2000: 27.
4. Margaret Prowse de Valle. *John Wesley: Un testimonio de vida* (John Wesley: A Life Testimony), in http://www.angelfire.com/pe/jorgebravo/wesley1.htm.
5. Prowse de Valle, (web site).
6. *The Works of Wesley,* Volume XI. Kansas City: Beacon Hill Press, 1986: 203-272, 521-523.
7. Clark, (web site).
8. Clark, (web site).
9. Prowse de Valle, (web site).

Lesson 8:

1. Rainer, Thom S. and Eric Geiger, *Simple Church,* B&H Publishing Group, 2006: 25-26.

Lesson 9:

1. Avery Willis y Steve Evans. *Making Disciples of Oral Learners.* Pattya, Tailandia: Lausanne Committee for World Evangelism & International Orality Network, 2005: 3. (www.lausanne.org/documents/2004forum/LOP54_IG25.pdf).

Lesson 10

1. Hull, 19 y 39.
2. Ogden, 23.
3. Hull, 14. Also in p. 19.
4. Ogden, 21.
5. Ogden, 24-37.
6. Hull, 25.
7. Hull, 25.
8. Hull, 25.
9. Hull, 29.
10. Hull, 35.
11. Hull, 28, 32.
12. Hull, 29, 40.
13. Rainer & Geiger, *Simple Church,* 26.

Appendices

Model of a Covenant for Group Discipleship No. 1

A DISCIPLE'S COVENANT

Greg Ogden, *Discipleship Essentials*, 14.

In order to grow towards maturity in Christ and complete Discipleship Essentials, I commit myself to the following standards:

1. Complete all assignments on a weekly basis prior to my discipleship appointment in order to contribute fully.

2. Meet weekly with my discipleship partners for approximately one and one-half hours to dialogue over the content of the assignments.

3. Offer myself fully to the Lord with the anticipation that I am entering a time of accelerated transformation during this discipleship period.

4. Contribute to a climate of honesty, trust and personal vulnerability in a spirit of mutual upbuliding.

5. Give serious consideration to continuing the discipling chain by committing myself to invest in at least two other people for the year following the initial completion of Discipleship Essentials.

Signed _____

Date _____

(The above commitments are the minimum standards of accountability, which are reviewed and renewed after various lessons. Feel free to add any other elements to your covenant.)

GROWTH GROUP COVENANT: COMMITMENT TO GROW IN CHRIST

Bill Hull, *The Disciple-Making Pastor*, 226-227.

Introduction: The following covenant sheet is to identify clearly the description of what is involved by joining a Growth Group. After attending our orientation meeting and prayerfully considering the challenge, opportunity and commitment, you need to sign this sheet and hand it in to our church office.

I. What is involved in a Growth Group?

- ✓ A desire to become a self-feeding Christian in prayer, accountable fellowship, the Word, and your witness.
- ✓ A willingness to come regularly to the meetings of the Growth Group and to always phone your Growth Group leader of potential absence.
- ✓ A commitment to be on time.
- ✓ A goal orientation to prepare all lessons in advance as part of your weekly devotional time with Christ.
- ✓ A willingness to place yourself under the leadership and direction of your Growth Group Leader's spiritual guidance.
- ✓ A determination to:
  1. Memorize 30 verses of Scripture in two years.
  2. Complete five Design for Discipleship Study books, one book analysis within the New Testament, and spiritual gift assessment for ministry.
  3. Write out and share your personal testimony.
  4. Aggressively cultivate friendships with the unchurched.
  5. Participate in all outreach events of your group and the church.
  6. And make prayer a regular part of your devotional life.

Covenant

After Reading these expectations I/we feel unworthy yet challenged to attempt what you have asked. I/we have prayed about this commitment and feel God is leading us to become Growth Group members. I/we desire to grow in pursuit of faith in Christ, love for others and the expansion of Christ's Kingdom. Therefore, I/we agree to channel our efforts to comply with these expectations for the next two years as God leads me/us. We give you permission to confront us whenever we fall short of this covenant as a friend and loving guide for our spiritual well-being.

Names:

Date:

Model of a Covenant for Group Discipleship No. 2

Example of a Basic Discipleship Training Weekend Program

	Thursday June 12	Friday June 13	Saturday
7:00 - 8:00		Breakfast/Devotional in Small Groups	Breakfast/Devotional in Small Groups
8:00 - 9:00		Worship	Worship
9:00 - 10:50		Discipleship as spiritual formation	How to develop a discipleship ministry
10:50 - 11:10		Break	Break
11:10 - 11:00		Discipleship as a means of multiplication and small groups	Meeting with leaders to work on a discipleship strategy
11:00 - 2:00		Lunch	
2:00 - 3:50	Worship/Introduction Break into small groups	Discipleship for everybody	
3:50 - 4:10	Break	Break	
4:10 - 6:00	What does it mean to be a disciple of Jesus?	Discipleship for pastors	
6:00 - 7:00	Dinner	Dinner	
7:00 - 8:45	Biblical foundations for discipleship	Discipleship strategy for the local church	
8:45 - 10:00	Discipleship in the family	Using discipleship materials	

EVALUATION SHEET

With the purpose of improving the quality of teaching the topics of this training and offering a better service through this ministry, we ask that you to be honest filling out this evaluation form.

Name: _____ Date: _____

Lesson: _____ Facilitator: _____.

Please respond to the items below using the following scale to evaluate:

V=Very good   G=Good   R=Regular   B=Bad

LESSON

1. Application to life themes ....V G R B
2. Met your expectations ....V G R B
3. Length of time of lesson ....V G R B
4. Useful tool for the Discipleship ministry ....V G R B

FACILITATOR

5. Level of knowledge of the topic shared ....V G R B
6. Interaction with participants ....V G R B
7. Answered your doubts satisfactorily ....V G R B
8. Widen my horizons, brought new light ....V G R B
9. Shared experiences about the topic ....V G R B
10. Proposed group activities ....V G R B
11. Punctuality and time management ....V G R B
12. Used a language that was easy to understand ....V G R B

MATERIAL

13. Visual material was clear and useful ....V G R B
14. Presentation of the printed material ....V G R B
15. Teaching material that was used ....V G R B
16. Recommendation of additional materials ....V G R B

SMALL GROUPS

17. Interchange with others ....V G R B
18. Fellowship that you experienced ....V G R B
19. Learning through discussions ....V G R B
20. Motivation to continue using groups ....V G R B

How would you apply what you have learned in this lesson personally and in your ministry?

We would appreciate your additional comments and suggestions.

Discipleship Training

Equipping disciples for the Mission

www.ingramcontent.com/pod-product-compliance
Lightning Source LLC
Chambersburg PA
CBHW080940040426
42444CB00015B/3390